THE
ANGER
DIET

THE ANGER DIET

THIRTY DAYS TO STRESS-FREE LIVING

Brenda Shoshanna, Ph.D.

Andrews McMeel
Publishing

Kansas City

06 07 08 09 RR4 10 9 8 7 6 5 4 3 2

ISBN-13: 978-0-7407-5492-0
ISBN-10: 0-7407-5492-0

Library of Congress Cataloging-in-Publication Data

Shoshanna, Brenda.
   The anger diet : thirty days to stress-free living / by
Brenda Shoshanna.
      p. cm.
   ISBN 0-7407-5492-0
   1. Anger. I. Title.

BF575.A5S48 2005
152.4'7—dc22

                                        2005040976

Book design by Pete Lippincott

ATTENTION: SCHOOLS AND BUSINESSES

Andrews McMeel books are available at quantity discounts with bulk purchase for educational, business, or sales promotional use. For information, please write to: Special Sales Department, Andrews McMeel Publishing, LLC, 4520 Main Street, Kansas City, Missouri 64111.

I dedicate this book to

Noah Lukeman,

without whose steadfast support, kindness, patience, inspiration, determination, and encouragement this book would never have come to life.

Contents

Contents

Contents

Acknowledgments

I WISH TO ACKNOWLEDGE AND THANK my wonderful editor, Dorothy O'Brien, and my ever-loving family and friends who have been there as a source of caring, understanding, and endless support. I thank Adam, Gerry, Melissa, Abram, Joshua, Yana, Jeff Asbell, Haskell Fleishaker, Ed Glassing, Martin Hara, Leslie Malin, Fran Perillo, Richard Schiffman, William Solomon, Carolyn Stark, Bernie Starr, Faye Tabakman, and Jacques Van Engel. I particularly acknowledge the wonderful contribution and inspiration of four beautiful children, Zoe, Remy, Jakey Bohrer, and Maya.

Introduction

May all beings have happiness and the causes of happiness.

— Buddhist prayer

EVERYONE WANTS TO BE BEAUTIFUL, young, healthy, and fit. There is no end to the diets, workouts, and health plans they can turn to in order to achieve these goals. Yet the most important diet of all has been overlooked. This is a diet that releases stress, relaxes muscles, offers sound sleep, diminishes appetite, and makes you look and feel younger—a diet that brings you new friends, a happy work environment, good relationships, and adds years to your life. This is the diet from anger—one of the worst plagues facing our nation.

Anger is a serious problem for one in every five Americans. Road rage, workplace violence, school shootings, domestic abuse, and addiction are just a few of its many expressions. The reason such a large number of our nation's citizens are on antidepressants, suffer from alcohol and drug addiction, are overweight, in broken relationships, and involved in all kinds of destructive behavior can be directly traced back to the effects of anger, particularly the hidden kind.

It is well documented that anger strongly affects physical health and is directly related to heart attacks, high blood pressure, back pain, and many other physical disorders.

When a symptom appears that is not the true cause of a problem, it is called symptom substitution.

We also turn our anger against ourselves in other ways. We become depressed or experience mood disorders, hopelessness, passive-aggressive behavior, promiscuity, domestic abuse, and many other forms of general misery. Sometimes anger converts itself into obsessive-compulsive disorders and individuals become unable to make decisions or choices about their lives.

Anger is ruthless in the course it takes, attacking and disrupting our body, mind, and spirit. As school and workplace shootings rise, the divorce rate climbs, and people are increasingly unable to deal with stresses such as those springing from 9/11 and other everyday threats, increasing numbers of people are on antidepressants. It is clear that anger is a societal problem that is only growing worse. It is time we paid attention to the number one terrorist we face: the anger we live with every day.

Society needs to address the problem of anger. We need a simple, clear-cut program that offers concrete psychological and spiritual tools for understanding and combating it. It is one thing to have an intellectual understanding of what is harmful. It is something else to know how to actually get rid of anger in your life. *The Anger Diet* will show you how.

The Anger Diet is a 30-day program that shows readers, day by day, how to let go of different forms of anger and replace it with healthy and constructive responses. Readers will receive a clear understanding of what anger is, how it works, when it appears, and why it camouflages itself and takes hold. They will also see the disastrous effects it has upon their lives and the lives of others—why it is so crucial to become anger-free.

The Anger Diet describes the 24 forms of anger and where they come from. The reader will learn how anger at your boss, anger at your spouse, anger at the government, and anger at yourself are all branches of one tree, growing from the same roots. The program shows how some people use anger as a defense, while others place anger at the core of their identity. The reader soon sees the toxicity of life lived with anger, and the joy of life without it.

The 30-day program offers day-to-day instructions and tips, along with practical techniques such as the Emergency Anger Technique, which teaches readers how to remain calm in the face of a storm.

Just as we work out daily in the gym to strengthen muscles and attain flexibility, readers can work out daily with the exercises in *The Anger Diet* to break harmful patterns. The exercises are simple and enjoyable, and readers will be able to see the fruits of their efforts immediately. Each day of the diet focuses on one form of anger that is to be given up that day, on what to replace it with, and on how to do it. Over the course of 30 days, the book systematically removes all the different forms of anger and replaces each one with an antidote. As we daily eliminate the toxicity anger places in our systems, the results will be reflected not only in our mental and emotional well-being but also in our environment and physical health. Eventually it will become impossible for anger to maintain the hold it now has on us.

Ultimately, it can be said that this is a book of forgiveness—forgiveness of self, of others, of God, and of the universe. Scriptures of all the world's religions enjoin us to be forgiving, but there is little actual instruction on how to accomplish this. Anger is the great impediment to forgiveness. When anger is rooted out, love and forgiveness arise naturally. Our lives and the lives of those around us then become hallowed and become all they are meant to be.

PART I

What Is Anger?

CHAPTER 1

The 24 Forms of Anger

As I have observed, those who plow trouble
and those who sow evil reap it.

—JOB 4:8 (New International Version)

AT THE PRESENT TIME large numbers of individuals in our society are dependent upon medication of all kinds. Antidepressants, anti-anxiety drugs, weight-loss supplements, medication to maintain low blood pressure, blood thinners, and antibiotics of many kinds are taken to ease the symptoms of unhappiness, unbalance, and disease we suffer from. On the face of it the symptoms seem to differ from one another. If we look a little deeper, however, we can see that beneath the various forms of distress that appear, anger is quietly smoldering.

Today we fear all kinds of external enemies. It is not so easy to realize, however, that the worst enemy we face is this anger that resides within, the terror it causes us, and the ways this poison affects so much of our lives.

Anger has many faces. It appears in various forms and creates different consequences. Anger that is overt is the simplest to deal with and understand. When we or someone we know is openly angry, we know what we are up against and can directly address the cause. Unfortunately, however, most anger lurks beneath the surface. It often does not even come to our awareness and manifests in endless, hidden ways—as depression, anxiety, apathy, hopelessness, and in myriad other forms.

It is crucial that we recognize anger for what it is, realize when it is appearing, and notice the devastation it creates. Then we have an opportunity to root out this underground stream that feeds the misery we feel, and the misery we cause others. When anger is allowed to remain camouflaged it holds us in its grip and easily erodes the quality of our entire lives.

Before we begin the diet to free ourselves of anger, we must become aware of the many ways anger attacks, how it camouflages itself, and the dances it does. By recognizing the 24 forms of anger, we will be able to shine a flashlight on the hidden enemy and begin the process of eliminating it from our lives.

The definitions of the 24 forms of anger are not set in stone and can vary somewhat from individual to individual. You will notice that many of the forms are interrelated, one giving rise to another. It's important to notice how anger works in your life. At the end of this chapter you will be given an opportunity to add your own forms of anger to the list.

To become aware is a wonderful beginning. Once your awareness grows strong and stable, you will no longer be a victim of anger's subtle attacks. You will also see clearly how impossible it is to live a healthy, fulfilling life when anger is living within you. As you stop indulging in the various forms of anger, you will inevitably become happier, healthier, stronger, more creative, more flexible, younger, and more fully alive.

The 24 Forms of Anger

1. *Straightforward Anger—Attack* This is anger that is clear-cut and easy to recognize. You feel angry and express it directly. Often the anger comes right out. Many regret it afterward, saying, "I was so angry, I couldn't control myself." This kind of anger has a life of its own; it rises like a flash storm and can easily turn into verbal, emotional, and physical abuse. When this kind of anger escalates it can lead to beatings, car crashes, accidents, murder, and wars of all kinds.

2. *Hypocrisy* You are angry and you know it, but you hide it beneath a smile and present a false persona, pretending to be someone you're not. You consciously behave in a way that hides who you really are and how you feel. This behavior evolves into hypocrisy and bad faith of all kinds. Although you think you are fooling others, in truth you are losing yourself and your own self-respect.

3. *Stealing—Taking That Which Has Not Been Given*
   This form of anger causes you to see yourself as being
   deprived, having less than others, and deserving to
   have what is theirs. Rather than being in touch with
   the natural abundance of life and ability to get what
   you need, you take it away from others. You envy their
   good fortune and seek to undo it. This form of anger
   refers to stealing material possessions as well as interfering with relationships others are enjoying that you
   feel you lack.

4. *Lying and Deception*   Lying and other forms of
   deception arise from anger and ill will. When this
   form of anger arises we fool another, harm, trick, or
   create confusion in their lives. This arises from lack of
   respect for oneself, for life, and for others. We are
   living a life based upon bad faith. However, when we
   fool others we also fool ourselves. Engaging in this
   behavior takes our own truth from us as well. Subtly or
   overtly, others lose their trust in us.

5. *Depression*   Depression is so pervasive these days that
   it may sometimes be difficult to recognize. There are
   the severe forms of depression, which disable an individual and are clear-cut. However, depression manifests in many other ways as well, as needing excessive
   sleep, lack of ability to concentrate, disturbing
   thoughts and dreams, difficulty eating, subtly harming

self and others, and in many other ways. Depression is anger and rage turned against oneself. It comes from not being able to identify or express (appropriately) the anger one is feeling. Although unacknowledged, the anger is there and in depression it turns against and attacks the person who is experiencing it.

6. *Withdrawal* Withdrawal is often a part of depression. It can arise from the fact that we do not feel "good enough." We cannot find our place in society or feel that we belong or can make a significant contribution of any kind. We feel shame and inadequacy, and we withdraw. When an individual is withdrawing, isolating themselves, or joining exclusive groups that are based upon hate or rejection of others, this is fueled by anger. The world and society at large are then viewed in a negative manner.

7. *Passive Aggression* Passive aggression is a form of anger expressed not by what we do but by what we do not do. An individual who is passive-aggressive knows exactly what the other person wants and needs, and simply does not do it. In this manner they upset and often enrage the other, while making it seem as though the other is overly demanding. This is a way of expressing anger without taking responsibility for it and at the same time blaming the other for outcomes of one's own behavior.

8. *Hopelessness* Hopelessness comes when we feel there is nothing we can do to handle the situation, emotions, or life we are living. The basic anger within destroys our innate sense of personal power, will, commitment, and ability to make a difference in the world. Hopelessness and despair can live inside an individual unrecognized. If they are present for too long, they often give rise to physical, mental, and emotional symptoms of all kinds. In order to heal these symptoms, it is often helpful to get back to the despair a person is feeling, and beneath that to the anger that is fueling this sense of impotence.

9. *Suicide and Suicidal Thoughts* Suicide, especially among young people, is more prevalent than ever today. As suicide and suicidal thoughts arise from feelings of hopelessness and despair, these feelings themselves are a direct expression of anger. Suicide is murder turned against oneself. Make no mistake, there is deep rage lying beneath this act and beneath the suicidal thoughts that accost an individual. Oddly enough, suicide often seems the only way to regain power, to get revenge on those who have hurt us, and also to get control over one's life and body. It is a way of pleading for attention that the suicidal person feels he or she cannot get in any other way. Pay close attention when suicidal ideas arise and persist. Even better

than that, stop this process before it starts. Learn how to uncover anger and root it out at its source.

10. *Burnout* Many individuals become exhausted and depleted either by their jobs or by relationships they are in. It becomes more and more difficult to experience enthusiasm, pleasure, and even the will to go on. At that time many feel that a rest, break, or renewal is the best cure for this feeling. Although these can be beneficial, it's important to note that the deepest cause of burnout is unacknowledged anger, which comes from frustration and insufficient rewards. Often, a person's dreams and goals have not been fulfilled and he or she grows tired of trying. Often, important communications the person has made have not been heard or responded to. It is necessary here to step back a moment and feel the anger underneath, to recognize the sense of being stopped and blocked in what one wants the most. When this is cleared out, appropriate action becomes clear and new forms of enthusiasm arise.

11. *Self-Sabotage* Self-sabotage is all too common in many forms. When things are going well at work or in relationships, many individuals sabotage themselves and their relationships in all kinds of subtle and unconscious ways. They stop their good from coming

their way. They create upset in those around them. They forget to take important actions that are required for their projects. They say things they do not mean. This is all unintended and arises from the deeper feeling that they do not deserve to succeed. They are punishing themselves, due to anger turned within.

12. *Low Self-Esteem*   When we see self-sabotage we also see low self-esteem. This is a lack of love, caring, and respect directed against the self. The low self-esteem is the result of anger. We have not pleased ourselves. Perhaps we have perfectionist standards. Perhaps we could not please important people in our lives when we were younger and still carry the bitter wounds around. Now we continue this negative behavior by thinking poorly of ourselves. We judge ourselves poorly. We find the worst in ourselves. We dwell upon our errors and imperfections. We quickly become our own worst enemy. Low self-esteem is the root cause of many other manifestations of anger that can become more and more severe.

13. *Compulsions*   Compulsions of all kinds can be thought of as defense mechanisms to bind the anxiety that arises from the anger we feel. When we carry a great deal of anger and it is unacceptable to us, we then need to find ways to avoid it, control it, and express it in hidden and distorted forms. Compulsions

then arise. We become compelled to perform certain acts. These acts can unconsciously become expiation for the guilt we feel about our own anger. The compulsions and the rituals that accompany them can also be symbolic expressions of the anger in acceptable ways. For instance, the compulsion many have to play violent video games is an acceptable way to express the violence and rage they suffer from within.

14. *Obsessions* Obsessions arise when we have a situation that we cannot resolve. There is something that has not been understood, come to terms with, or completed. We refuse to let the situation go. Often the energy that keeps obsession going is anger or revenge. When we find ourselves thinking about the same situation or person over and over, we see that there has been a wound to the individual and release and forgiveness are needed. If we cannot forgive the person who has wounded us, the obsession with the injury done us can easily consume our lives.

15. *Desire for Revenge* Revenge and revenge fantasies are, unfortunately, very common. When individuals have been hurt or wounded, they believe that the way to heal their wound and restore justice is by harming the other person equally. In this way they descend to the other's level and become gripped by anger and rage. Holding on to thoughts of revenge is holding on to

poison. Not only does the anger grow and affect a person's entire system, but even if one is able to exact the revenge they desire, it often is unfulfilling. And then, as a result of dwelling upon hate and anger, it is easy to attract more of that in your life.

16. *Addictions* We often become addicted to various substances as a way of numbing our feelings and blocking out anger. Through addiction we give ourselves what feels like pleasure, security, or safety, though it is temporary. The more we cling to the addiction, the more of it we need, and the more intense the feelings, which are rumbling beneath the surface, become as well.

We can also become addicted to anger. For some anger is a substance that gives a false sense of power, security, safety, and control. Anger becomes who they are and characterizes their way of walking in the world. However, just as with any addiction, there is a tremendous price to pay. And these feelings of power and strength are only illusory. When real power, strength, and understanding are needed, anger cannot provide them at all.

17. *Psychosomatic Disorders* For many individuals anger becomes expressed through bodily symptoms, creating all kinds of aches, pains, and diminution of well-being. The mind-body connection is being increasingly

studied, and shows that the accumulation of unacknowledged anger leads to high blood pressure, physical stress, heart disorders, back pain, and many, many other physical symptoms. It is impossible to live in a state of anger and frustration and not have it affect our flesh, blood, and bones. Along with vitamins, good diet, and exercise, flushing anger out of one's system is a must for ongoing health.

18. *Catastrophic Expectations* Some individuals live their lives in terror and fear. They are always expecting something awful to happen, seeking problems, and dwelling upon danger, and are unable to shake the sense that they are vulnerable to the random chaos of the world. This is the basis of terrorism. Once the seeds of fear are planted inside the human being, once they can be made to expect catastrophe, the entire fabric of their life alters.

Some become unable to recognize that most of these feared catastrophes never come to pass. Such fears are thoughts that have taken over our lives. These catastrophic expectations are based upon exaggeration and a sense of helplessness. (This is not to say that healthy awareness of danger is not needed. But when it becomes exaggerated and takes over one's life it is something else).

Catastrophic expectations arise from a feeling of powerlessness and from dwelling upon thoughts and images in one's mind rather than being directly in the present moment. These expectations arise from a loss of faith in oneself, from not being in touch with one's natural ability to handle situations as they arise. This is a form of anger turned against the self.

19. *Masochism*　Masochism is a condition of actually taking pleasure in pain that is caused to oneself. The masochist consciously or unconsciously enjoys suffering. Pain and humiliation are associated with pleasure, or victory. Oftentimes masochists have been hurt and humiliated as children. By consciously looking for and enjoying hurtful situations now, they are seeking to take control of what happened in the past. Unconsciously they are saying to their tormentors, "You cannot hurt me any longer, because now I am doing it to myself." Masochists look for relationships, projects, or situations where they can suffer or fail. Sexual masochists take sexual pleasure in being hurt, degraded, and humiliated. Their entire lives become an expression of hatred, punishment, and anger turned toward the self and also others, those who are tormenting them now.

20. *Sadism*　Sadists take active pleasure in hurting others and seeing the pain they cause. This gives them a sense of power, importance, and control. The basis of sadism is weakness and a feeling of inner impotence.

The only way sadists can overcome this is by controlling or harming someone else. Sadism expresses itself in many, many ways, including in abusive relationships, where an individual becomes hurtful, dominating, possessive, and overly demanding in many ways. Sadism is a direct expression of anger. It has taken over the individual's life.

21. *Martyrdom—Causing Guilt* The martyr enjoys making others feel guilty, obligated, and wrong. Martyrs often act like saints, seeming to give selflessly. Their entire persona cries out, "I'm so wonderful and faultless and look what you've done to me." You will find the martyr giving and giving without receiving a proper return or recognition. The return the martyr receives is the pleasure of making another feel less than them and guilty.

   This is a devious expression of anger and of manipulating and obligating others. Be careful and aware around these individuals. When you are with a person and feel overly obligated to them, less than them, or guilty about them, the other person's behavior is rooted in anger with you, being expressed in this underhanded way.

22. *Being Critical, Judgmental* Some people are constantly judgmental and critical of others (and often of themselves). They always look for what is wrong or

missing in a situation. It is almost impossible for some of these individuals to be pleased, or to find anything good. Some are perfectionists, setting impossible standards for themselves and others to meet. Some parents engage in this behavior with their children, thinking they are being helpful to them. It is not difficult to see, however, that this kind of behavior is an expression of anger, coated in a socially approved fashion, seeming to urge another on to what is best for them. One must realize, however, that they can never bring out the best in another by always looking for what is wrong.

23. *Blaming* Blame is different from criticism. Critical people are always looking for something wrong. Blame is the active projection of all that is wrong in a relationship or in one's life upon another person. Those who blame cannot or will not take responsibility for anything or see their part in it. They use blame to hide from who they are and from their own failings. Blame is a direct attack upon another person and should be recognized as such. It is also an attack upon the truth. The truth is that if you want to change or heal a situation, instead of blaming someone else, look and see where your own part lay. Look at the choices you have made and where you can now change.

24. *Gossiping* Gossiping is one of the most common activities of our day; it is also one of the most

dangerous and lethal. We gossip for fun, and during this activity discuss negative aspects of a person or things they've done that are questionable. This naturally interferes with the relationship between the person we are talking about and those who hear the gossip. Gossip also spreads, becomes distorted, tears down the person's reputation, and can easily grow into slander. Not only does it harm the one gossiped about, but those who are gossiping are silently sending poison, bathing in anger and hate.

YOUR OWN FORMS OF ANGER

Write down some ways that anger manifests in your life. Take time with this. Notice it day by day. Just writing it down, describing it for what it is, will begin the process of undoing anger's harmful effects. In the process you may also want to note what is causing the anger. Most individuals have only a dim recognition of what it is that truly upsets them. Don't censor yourself in the process. You do not have to be rational or self-critical. Odd things can cause different reactions. Just use this time to look and see.

Nonviolence is a weapon of the strong.

— MAHATMA GANDHI

CHAPTER 2

The Addiction to Anger

*In my mind are thoughts that can hurt or help me. I am
constantly choosing the contents of my mind.*

— Dr. Gerald Jampolsky, *Love Is Letting Go of Fear*

It is easy to become addicted. Addiction is a complex process, which is built into human experience in many ways. We are all creatures of habit. Habits and routines provide a sense of certainty, security, and stability in our lives. Many identify themselves with these routines and habits. When they are disrupted their sense of well-being becomes threatened.

When we depend upon a habit for our sense of well-being, it is easy for this habit to develop into an addiction. We feel that without this particular habit (action, feeling, substance, or person), we cannot get by. Anxiety develops, and we begin to crave feeling good again. Before we know it, we will do anything to fulfill this craving. At this point we are dependent upon the habit, associating it with our well-being and using it in a way it was not intended for. Along with habits, we can become addicted to anything: dreams, fantasies, people, feelings, activities—whatever brings relief to us.

By now our habit has turned into an addiction and prevents us from living freely. We feel we cannot go forward without our habit. Our choices, actions, and relationships can be taken over by it. Although we feel good for a short while, the consequences of addictions—the price we pay for them—are vast and usually unrecognized.

There are many ways of being addicted and many purposes an addiction serves. Addiction to anger is one of the most common and lethal addictions, and one of the most seldom recognized. Like addiction to alcohol or drugs, the addict feels good in the beginning and becomes hooked by anger, and then, gradually, as the addiction grows, it consumes more and more of their life, producing painful consequences.

The best way to undo an addiction is to look it squarely in the face, see how it operates, when it arises, how it maneuvers, the lies it tells us, the false promises it offers, and the huge costs we pay for it. Once we understand the process of addiction fully, the next step is to undo the fear that keeps it going—to handle the underlying need that fuels it. In this way we take back the power over our own lives.

To begin this process, we will look at some of the functions addiction serves.

The Functions of Addictions

When we are addicted, all we can think about is our addiction, about getting another "hit." Our focus and attention narrow, and many aspects of life are blocked out. This itself is soothing to many. As focus narrows it numbs us and blocks out painful feelings and experiences that we may not wish to deal with. At this point the addiction is serving as a defense against pain and anxiety. It is preventing us from seeing and dealing with issues that need to be attended to. Although this presents temporary relief, the situation behind the addiction, the fuel that feeds it, festers and intensifies.

Addictions also provide a sense of pleasure, power, of being high, mighty, and invincible (a defense against the feelings of helplessness and inadequacy many feel). Despite the fact that these good feelings the addiction produces are temporary, the craving for them can become so intense that the person becomes blind to the consequences of their addiction. They also become blind to the fact that as the addiction develops, the dosage increases— they inevitably require more and more of the addictive substance or behavior to feel okay. As the dosage increases, so does the addiction's negative impact on their life. Many become slaves to their addiction. Little by little it takes everything away.

Addiction provides a false sense of security. All the while an addiction is running, it makes the individual feel safe and secure. The reality, however, is that those addictions destroy an individual's true safety. It blinds him from doing what needs to be done to build a life of true value and stability.

Lenny was usually a mild-mannered man who withdrew when faced with conflict and troubling situations. He feared speaking up, feared hurting others, and feared being in the wrong. As a result, his work life suffered. He was passed over for promotions and, despite his fine skills, was relegated to lower-level tasks. During one office conflict, when his immediate boss was present, something inside Lenny flipped over. "I couldn't take it anymore," he said. "I felt my face get red and then just opened my mouth and let everyone know where I stood in no uncertain terms." To Lenny's amazement, rather than being censored for his outburst, he was respected. People started to look at him with new eyes, as someone to be reckoned with.

This was Lenny's first experience with anger. He liked it. It provided a sense of power and strength that had been lacking. Afterward he felt better as well. Soon he became hooked. Rather than deal with his feelings about himself and learn constructive ways of relating to others, Lenny began to depend upon having outbursts (the way children may depend on having tantrums). Lenny's outbursts stopped his coworkers in their tracks, dominated the situation, and gained him the attention he had long desired. Soon Lenny began trying this at home as well. Despite the upset he generated around him, he got what he wanted.

Effects of Addiction to Anger

Before long Lenny was addicted to anger. In the beginning it gave him a feeling of strength. He didn't even notice that his closer friends and family were withdrawing from him. He didn't connect the anger with the new difficulty he'd developed with his digestion or the bad dreams he was having. Lenny soon began to feel that without the anger he would be vulnerable, used, passed by. He needed the anger for his very life. And he was willing to pay the price.

When we are angry we often have a temporary feeling of strength, energy, righteousness, power, authority, or control. Much like alcohol, the surge of anger that takes over can block out fears, inhibitions, and doubts. There is a temporary sense of freedom and empowerment that we normally lack.

Anger can also block out logical thought processes, producing a sense that we are absolutely right. When some are angry there is no room for wavering, and they feel no need to. Some individuals who have trouble making decisions can make them easily then. They do not realize that it is not *they* who are making the decisions, but the anger they are host to. Decisions made while angry are often unilateral and focus only upon a limited aspect of the entire situation. These kinds of decisions rarely lead to positive outcomes.

Anger provides a sense of justification. Many actions that might seem unacceptable when we are calm seem perfectly fine when we are angry. Anger also encourages us to blurt out negative thoughts and feelings we may have been holding in that might better have been left unsaid. Of course, after the surge of anger passes, it is difficult to take these words back. Even if we apologize, the after-effects remain. Although it might have felt good to speak out while angry, a little later on, when reality dawns, there is often a sense of regret. In one way or another we have to pay for what we have done.

Anger Diet Preparation

The exercises offered in the introductory chapters can be considered preparation for the Anger Diet itself. They place the subject of anger in a larger context and give us some time to till the soil of our minds and hearts—to understand the need for and get ready to embark upon the actual diet itself. Though simple, these exercises are powerful and effective. They will help you look into your life and begin the process of uprooting the anger within.

Preparation 1
AUTOMATIC ANGER

List the times when you feel angry or upset automatically. What persons, thoughts, memories, or situations bring this up? For now, just notice this and write it down. As you go through the day, if another one strikes you, step back and notice it, and write it down as well. Rather than reacting blindly, we are taking time here to just look.

CHAPTER 3

Anger as Identity

Who would I be without my anger?

UNFORTUNATELY, the anger many individuals live with on a daily basis can become crystallized as part of their identity—a tough guy, a bully, a smart aleck, a warrior, a martyr, and so on. This identity that they assume becomes an armor around them, justifying them in their anger and also protecting them from retribution from others. Once this identity becomes habitual and set in stone, the individuals forget it is something they have taken on, much as an actor plays a role onstage. They begin to feel it is who they truly are and soon have no idea who they would be without it. This false entity then blocks out much of the happiness, flexibility, communication, and intimacy they desire.

"Who would I be without my anger?" Roger asked, and then answered in the same breath. "I'd be mush, putty, someone anyone could step all over." Roger was in therapy with his wife, trying to deal with problems in his marriage. His first response was always to be the tough guy, to defend himself from accusations.

"I'm not letting her walk all over me," he'd balk whenever she expressed her needs or upset. Rather than listening to what his wife said he immediately took her words as criticism. "Is she trying to tell me I'm inadequate?" he'd demand. The war was on. What started as a conversation turned into a power struggle. From Roger's point of view his very life was at stake here. He felt he had to protect his identity as a man at all costs. "I'm a tough guy," he said over and over.

However, as long as Roger held on to his identity as "a tough guy" there was no hope of working through the problems in his marriage or of his even really understanding what was going on. His strong identification with being tough prevented him from listening, reaching out, or realizing that his wife's needs and feelings might have nothing at all to do with him. He wasn't available to finding a solution or to allowing the truth of his own self to come through. These are some of the consequences when anger, fear, and self-justification turn into our sense of who we are.

Unfortunately, some of the identities that anger hides behind are socially approved, applauded, and encouraged. In some circles it is considered wonderful to be so competitive and ambitious that you'll do anything to win and climb the ladder. It may not matter how many people's throats get cut along the way, or how much damage is done in the process. The winner takes all and receives admiration, applause, or adulation.

However, thinking "I am a winner" and identifying with that label creates another false sense of oneself. As a "winner" an individual feels powerful, and better and stronger than others. As the winner he blocks out the reality of what he may have done to get there, or the effects his actions may have had on others.

There are other drawbacks as well. When we identify with a role, title, or label there is never a long-term sense of security. Soon someone comes along to challenge the title and the winner then becomes anxious and fearful of losing her fragile title, fearful of turning into the loser and of losing her temporary sense of herself.

Beyond that, it is impossible not to receive the fruits of what you have put forth. "As you sow, so shall you reap" is an immutable law of life. Although we may justify all kinds of behavior under the guise of being the winner, a tough guy, or whatever, it is absolutely inevitable that we will experience the consequences of our thoughts, actions, and deeds. The false sense of identity blinds us to this temporarily, and this is a danger we must recognize. This is why it is so very important to be in touch, moment by moment, with the full context of the situation we are living in.

Identities Anger Assumes

Following are some other ways in which anger cloaks and expresses itself and some of the ways in which these different identities play themselves out. You may be surprised to notice some identities that you have either taken on or been at the effect of—the controller, the tease, the helpless person, the martyr or victim, the perfect person (perfectionist), the power broker, and the intrusive and overly solicitous friend. Add some of your own roles to the list and take a moment to see their effects.

The Controller

The controller may appear to have extra strength, knowledge, and the ability to take charge. Many are willing to have controllers take over and lead them to success. On the surface it seems beneficial and the controller may argue that he controls you for your own ultimate good—he only wants the best for all concerned. While this may be true on one level, it is *the controller's* idea of what is good for you that you are succumbing to. In this way those being controlled relinquish their sense of themselves and what is right for them.

There are other prices to be paid for this as well. When one feels he must or can control others, beneath this attitude lies disrespect based on a conviction that others are not up to taking charge of their own lives and can be moved around according to the controller's wishes. Not only does the controller fail to see the best in others but he or she is also relating to others as objects rather than as equals. The implicit message controllers give is that they are better or wiser or stronger than you and that you *need* them. This fosters a sense of both dependency and inadequacy. It creates a feeling in others that they lack the ability to make their own choices or use their own natural abilities. It is never healthy to be controlled, no matter how weak we may feel. The greatest kindness anyone can give you is to help you find the strength within to stand on your own two feet.

The Tease

Another example of anger assuming a different identity is the tease. A tease may also be called a flirt, charmer, or seducer—in the most extreme form, the con man. These individuals are charming, delightful, full of smiles. You feel good in their presence. Some exude a charisma that creates a feeling of happiness and excitement within. The tease offers you something that stirs your heart, entices your imagination, lures you. Whether spoken or unspoken a promise is being made.

But how often is this promise fulfilled? What is it that the tease is asking for in exchange for this promise they are offering? So many people pay well up front, only to find themselves left empty-handed.

The tease is playing games with you. They enjoy their power of seduction, which gives them a sense of value and strength. Some also enjoy not coming through. They have gotten the better of you. This makes them feel better, smarter, more in charge. There is anger underneath this. These individuals are playing cat and mouse.

Each identity that is motivated by anger has a different scenario. When we are in direct touch with our own nature, when we are free of being trapped by our own anger, we can see things for what they are, and not get caught by the games others play.

Preparation 2
TAKING THE MASK OFF

1. List some roles you play that are fueled by anger. Write out the ways in which this plays out with others. Just take a look at what happens, without self-blame.
2. List some ways you are caught by the roles played by others. Again, write out the ways in which this happens. Take time to let it sink in.
3. Write out a little scenario for each of these roles. Take time to see what messages, requests, demands, and attitudes you are giving out and receiving as well. Are they healthy for you and those you interact with?

This exercise may seem more difficult than it is. Just do it step by step. New thoughts and ideas about it will come to you day by day. As you are simply living your life, insight and awareness will also arrive.

CHAPTER 4

The Emergency Technique

*He who is slow to anger is better than a strong man—
a master of his passions is better than a conqueror of a city.*

— Ben Zoma, Jewish scripture

WHEN WE ARE IN THE MIDST OF ANGER, our natural reaction is to blame, attack, or wish the offender ill in some way. Not only is this harmful to others and ourselves, but it keeps the anger growing stronger, and never ultimately solves the problem—in fact, it usually makes it worse.

The Emergency Technique is an important tool to have at your disposal the next time an angry situation arises. It will be hard to use this technique while you are caught in the grip of anger unless you've mastered it beforehand. So study it now, and practice it. Once you've made the technique your own, you can use it more effectively during an emergency. If you have a hard time grasping it or practicing it now, visualize an individual or situation that recently made you angry, something that still burns hot for you.

There are a lot of steps here, and while in the grip of anger you might not be able to recall them all. That's okay. Utilizing even one of these steps can make a huge difference.

Steps of the Emergency Technique

1. The moment you notice anger rising in you, stop everything. Stand or sit completely still. (Anger often expresses itself in the body, too.) Breathe deeply. Become as silent as you can. Count your breaths until you reach 10.

2. Put this situation in the largest possible context, in the context of your entire life. Realize that whatever is at stake, it is not the end of the world.

3. Allow for the possibility that you are in the wrong. As anger starts to build, your mind will give you a thousand reasons why you are right and the other is wrong, why you have a right to be angry. Everything in society encourages us to be angry, to get back at others, not to be a doormat, to get what is right for us. Realize that while in the midst of anger, we can never clearly see or know the entire situation. Realize that the other party has his or her own perspective, and feels as justified as you. Pretend, just for now, that the other party might actually be in the right. Tell yourself that you don't always have to be right; that there is plenty of time in life to be in the right, and that you can be right another time.

4. Remind yourself that the other person is not necessarily trying to do you ill. Realize that anger is all

about how you perceive the situation, about the story you tell yourself about what is happening. But this is not necessarily what is happening at all. Realize that a lot of the time anger breeds paranoia, and that we are angry mostly because we think that the other party wishes us ill, or is deliberately trying to anger us. Tell yourself that the other person might also think that you are trying to do him ill, and might merely be defending himself from you. Now go even further and picture that the person is actually trying to help you, has done whatever he has done for your own good, even if it doesn't seem like it.

5. Imagine something that would make you feel compassion for the other party, for instance, that the other party is suffering tremendously. When we feel compassion for someone, it is impossible to be angry with him or her.

6. Forgive the other person for having made you angry.

7. Forgive yourself for having been angry, and for having acted however you did.

8. Think of a way you could turn the situation around and make an enemy into a friend. Think of a way you can actually help this person. Do it.

At a certain point, you will inevitably notice that something deep within you has settled down. A calm may take over, a sense of well-being. Sometimes the person or situation responds very quickly and things turn around on their own. But whether or not this happens, you will feel good; when you think of the situation or person later on, you will not have any clean-up to do. At the very least all will be neutralized—at the most you will feel renewed love.

This technique is foolproof and can be done anywhere, anytime.

Case Study

Marcia was in an abusive marriage with a dominating husband. Whenever he walked into the room and started to demand things of her, she felt helpless to resist, and also felt worthless. When we explored the way Marcia perceived her husband, it became clear that she saw him as powerful, successful, smart, and in control, and saw herself as the opposite. The moment she saw him, these feelings automatically took root.

In order to get quick control of this automatic reaction, we simply changed the way Marcia perceived him. Although he dressed impeccably and was overbearing, Marcia decided to view him as someone who had just returned from the hospital and had had electric shock treatments. She pictured that the treatments were causing his insolence and anger toward her, and that his behavior did not reflect upon her in any way.

The next time her husband began to behave that way, Marcia saw him with that adjustment, as if she were in a play. He then no longer had the power to frighten her. Instead, she felt sorry for him and just smiled. The pattern had broken. Marcia felt her own power. She realized that she had given him the power he had had over her by the way she had chosen to perceive him. When this was adjusted, little by little the two of them were able to create a much more level playing field.

In actuality, no matter how badly a person may have behaved, he or she always has positive qualities as well. Later on, when you are calmer, you can think about these. As Marcia and her husband began to adjust their relationship, she did not necessarily maintain her initial fiction about him, but opened her mind to see both him and herself more realistically. But for the purpose of making use of the Emergency Technique to break intransigent patterns, it is necessary to quickly refocus your thoughts and place attention on whatever it is that calms you down and alters the balance. What's most important here is not allowing the usual inner dialogue to roll.

PART II

The Anger Diet

CHAPTER 5

Overview of the Anger Diet

WELCOME TO THE ANGER DIET. This section of the book presents a 30-day plan in which you will learn to take control of your life and diminish your anger greatly and enjoyably.

Each day's plan deals with a different form of anger. Each chapter covers one day, one form of anger, and explains that particular form of anger, so that you have a full understanding of where this anger comes from and the different ways it manifests in your life. You will also see the ways in which this form of anger affects you. For each form of anger you are given specific directions and exercises about how to recognize it and stop it from taking charge.

An antidote is given to take the place of the anger. Just as in a regular diet you might replace a piece of cake with a piece of fruit, we will offer specific replacements for the particular form of anger we are exploring. Then when this form of anger arises, instead of immediately being caught by it, you quickly do the exercise and use the antidote.

When you are caught by anger and react automatically, distress arises and expresses itself in your life and body. When you have the power of awareness, your attention becomes freed from negativity and you have choice over how you think, feel, and respond. Then natural health, wisdom, and goodwill are yours.

A wonderful feature of this diet is that results are noticeable immediately. The more you practice the diet, the more faithfully you stay on it, the more quickly and fully a new life dawns.

Some of the chapters, some of the forms of anger, will be more difficult than others for you to handle. This is to be expected. You may experience resistance. Don't worry about it. Just follow the simple directions for that day, no matter how you feel. As we make changes in our usual habits and routines, it is natural to experience various forms of upset or resistance. This is simply the habitual energy trying to keep itself alive. If you do not make it too important or allow it to stop you, the resistance or upset will dwindle away on its own.

Some chapters will be more meaningful for you than others. This is also to be expected. Different individuals are susceptible to different forms of anger. Go through each chapter anyhow. As you do this, you may find many surprises about yourself and you may also learn a great deal about others in your world.

If you miss a day, don't skip a chapter or two. Simply resume where you left off. Some individuals may want or need to take more time on a chapter, or pause a little between them. Don't be rigid about it and don't make yourself wrong. Just go along day by day as best you can. Even one day's work, even one chapter fully done, has the power to change your life. Each chapter contains a wealth of material, an actual feast. It's best, however, to take just one bite at a time and chew thoroughly.

As you start on the program, you are learning new life-enhancing techniques. Once you make the technique your own, you will use it again and again. Of course, the more you use it, the simpler and more automatic the new technique will become.

Every few days, a chapter and a day is devoted to "Review and Repair." This is an extremely important day. It is a time for integration, and for repairing any damage that may have been done to yourself or others by one of the forms of anger you have been working on eliminating. Some find this day too short. They want to do the "Review and Repair" for a few days. That's fine. If you feel you need more time to integrate and practice what you've learned, take more time. It can take time for new ideas to work their way into your consciousness. Remember, we all have different rhythms, and they are to be respected. Be kind and patient with yourself. This is the best antidote of all.

As you begin actually doing the exercises the ideas will take hold more quickly. Taking action on a new idea is the best way to make it your own.

Most important of all, please enjoy the journey. This diet is not meant to be heavy or filled with self-righteousness. Guilt is not an ingredient we use at all. There is also no room in the diet for punishment—of self or others.

A wonderful way to go through this process and make it your own is to join together with others who are on the same journey. It's wonderful to give and receive support, and to find like-minded companions on the road.

Grudges

*To be wronged or robbed is nothing,
unless you continue to remember it.*

— CONFUCIUS

ONE DAY SANDRA DISCOVERED that her best friend of many years, Nina, had been speaking about her behind her back. Not only had she been speaking about her, but she had actually lied to her to her face. The person she had thought was closer than a sister was actually two-faced and could not be trusted.

Sandra was devastated. Not only did she cut off her friendship with Nina, but she began to doubt her own judgment. This doubt spread and finally grew into a general lack of trust. Sandra's life became embittered.

After some time passed, Nina attempted to contact her, but Sandra would have none of it. She had firmly decided to never let this person back into her life. She had also firmly decided never to talk it out or listen to what happened from Nina's point of view. As far as Sandra was concerned, reconciliation was impossible. In her mind,

Nina was dead. Clearly, Sandra was holding a deep, immovable grudge.

The Nature of a Grudge

Grudges are so common in our lives that we rarely consider that there is anything wrong with holding one. When someone does us wrong (or we think that someone has done us wrong), it seems natural to close our hearts, to put up a wall. We have become the judge and jury, with no chance of appeal.

And when we tell the story about what the person has done to us (as we do over and over to friends), others usually agree adamantly. We have been misused. We have every reason to stay angry with this person. We have every reason to hate him, discard him, see the worst about him. After all, the person has wronged us. It is smart to drop such a person from our lives. It is insurance that we will never be hurt by him again. But this kind of insurance is expensive. We do not realize how much we pay for it. We also do not realize that by holding on to grudges, we are doing the thing we fear most: inflicting hurt upon ourselves.

Each grudge we hold on to creates a callus on our heart. It hardens us, closes up the easy flow between us and all of life. If something new and wonderful appears in our lives, we are not free to partake of it. Our grudge is like a little time bomb, feeding us thoughts of fear, souring our feelings about others, causing us to become distrustful and to miss out on a lot of good.

In addition, it is extremely important to realize that the principle of *self-fulfilling prophecies* operates here as well. If you dwell upon something, if you expect it to happen and see it happening, guess what? You will draw it to you. If you are dwelling upon how you've been hurt or misused by someone, inevitably you draw those kinds of experiences into your life. Soon it looks like the whole world is filled with users and liars out to hurt you. Your seemingly harmless grudge has done this to you. It has succeeded in narrowing your vision and drawing the worst to you.

How We Keep Grudges Going

We keep grudges going in several ways. First, we keep them alive by dwelling upon them. This gives the grudge importance and energy, and makes it a big part of our lives. Although we may think we have discarded the person, or no longer see her, she actually becomes *more* central to us, since we are dwelling upon her and the wrong she's done. This keeps her very close at hand, with us every day.

Second, we keep grudges going by our false belief that they are harmless. But grudges are not at all harmless; they always reverberate upon the one who holds them.

Third, we keep grudges alive by believing they are justified, that we are in the right for keeping them, and that if we let them go, we would be a fool. We wonder how could we live without our grudges to protect us. The real question is, how do we live *with* them?

Unconscious Grudges

Believe it or not, it is possible to hold on to a grudge without realizing that we are doing so. Many individuals are out of touch with their feelings. They are unaware of their reaction at the time something happens. Some words may have passed between them and another person, perhaps a misunderstanding that was not corrected. Although on the surface they may have let it go by as though it were nothing, silently and unconsciously they formed a grudge. Unfortunately, this all happened so quickly that these individuals have no way of recognizing what was truly going on. All they may have been aware of was a feeling of hurt or discomfort. Perhaps they realized they were withdrawing, but gave the whole matter little further thought.

Unaware of the power of a grudge and how it destroys relationships, when that person comes to mind this individual might now make excuses as to why they are no longer interested in being that person's friend. They might think that they just somehow lost interest, that the person has suddenly become boring or burdensome. They simply have no desire to return that person's calls. Such an individual does not recognize that they have developed a grudge.

Like a pit that gets stuck in your throat when swallowing, a grudge lodges in your heart and mind and prevents natural relations with the person you have a grudge against.

Today's Diet
GIVE UP ONE GRUDGE

The following exercise, like all the exercises in this book, is simple. Don't make it more complicated than it is. Just follow directions. Daily awareness practice has the ability to dislodge much confusion and sorrow that we've held on to for years. You are not being asked to do anything more right now than become aware. Awareness itself is a powerful agent that makes change happen on its own.

STEP 1: *Make a List of Those You Hold Grudges Against.*

Your list may surprise you, but don't worry about it. Just write down anyone you can think of.

STEP 2: *Write Down What Each Person Did to Cause You to Develop the Grudge.*

This part is also fascinating. Sometimes you'll find that the same thing was done to you many times by many different people. Other times you'll notice that a whole array of different things causes you to close your heart. Don't judge yourself or the other person as you write. Just put it all down. This is a time for exploration.

STEP 3: *Write Down How Long You've Held This Grudge.*

This is also intriguing. Some people will find that they've held a grudge for 20 years, others just a few months or a day. Notice your capacity for freezing time and action. When we hold a grudge for such a long time, we implicitly say that nothing changes, that we haven't grown nor has the other person; what was so important at one time still means the same to us now.

For example, one woman noticed she had held a grudge for years and years against her first boyfriend because he took her friend and not her to the senior prom. At the time she felt devastated. Now, as the mother of three, with years of growth and experience, when she realized this she stopped and asked herself if she thought this was as devastating now as she thought it was then. Her reaction now was different; she paused and wondered why he had made that choice. Then she suddenly realized that she had been leaving to go far away to college and her boyfriend had been quite hurt about it. He was frightened about losing her, and so chose someone else. He was starting the process of separation. Although she still didn't think it was a wise choice, it no longer upset her as it once had. Most of us hold on to old wounds as though they happened yesterday, without taking the time to look at them clearly in the light of who we are now, what we have learned, what is currently important to us.

STEP 4: *Grudge Replacement.*

1. Go over your list. Write down one thing you liked about each person you have a grudge against. Or write down one kind thing that that person has done for you.

2. Go over your list of the reasons you developed a grudge. For every reason you created a grudge, write down one time you behaved that way. If possible, note your reasons for that behavior. See if you still think this behavior is so unforgivable.

3. Now, notice once again how long you've held on to this grudge. Write down the consequences of holding on to this—what did you lose as a result of it? (If you can't think of an answer at first, just reflect upon this. An answer may come on its own later on.)

STEP 5: *Repair the Grudge.*

1. Ask yourself what you would need in order to let go of each grudge. Take time with this one. An answer may not come right away. If it doesn't, be patient. If you continue to return to this part of the exercise, sooner or later an answer will appear. If you do get an answer, ask yourself if you would be willing to let go of the grudge if you got what you needed. Also check to see whether what you think you need is extreme. Are you setting up barriers, making things impossible?

2. Ask yourself whether you are willing to ask for what you need from the person who hurt you. If so, do it at once, the sooner the better. The longer you think about it, the less likely it is to happen.

3. Once it does happen, both of you may be delighted, and you very well may also discover the other person had no idea why (or indeed that you were) holding a grudge. They may have just sensed the distance and been confused about it.

This step of asking for what you need to repair the hurt might be easy for some and almost impossible for others. Don't worry. It is not absolutely essential to do this, though it can help quite a lot.

LET GO OF ONE GRUDGE A DAY

Some have a short list of grudges, others' lists are very long. Our ultimate wish is to get rid of all of them. Letting go of one grudge a day may be too much for some people, or not enough for others. If it's too much, then do as much as you can. Let go of one grudge a week, or a month. When you let go of one grudge, several others may unknowingly fall away as well. You'll notice how much lighter you feel. Your health will improve, your waistline will decrease, and your life will proceed much more easily.

Judging Others

Judge everyone favorably; this promotes peace.

— RASHI

NO MATTER WHOM SHE MET, the first reaction Barbara had was to search for faults in the person. As soon as she was introduced, she'd look the person over and pinpoint where trouble spots lay. First she'd begin asking subtle questions to find out more about their life, where had they gone to school, had they been married, what kind of work did they do?

"I want to know who I'm up against," Barbara said, explaining herself. "I don't take people at face value. I learned that a long time ago."

Clearly Barbara felt that she had been fooled, tricked, and taken in when she was trusting. Now she'd built this defense around herself to prevent herself from getting hurt. This identity that she assumed of the judge also served other purposes for her. It also had other consequences.

By immediately judging others, Barbara was also assessing how she measured up. Her basic orientation was competitive. She saw others as opponents. By finding all these faults with them, she was simultaneously elevating herself, bolstering her sense of self-esteem, assuring herself that she had the ability to handle the interaction and stay on top.

The Nature of Judging Others

What Barbara did not realize was that as she judged others so she was also judged. Whatever we see in others we simultaneously see in ourselves. We also inevitably draw to us people who see us in the same way.

Barbara was also creating distance between herself and others. She was eliminating a basic sense of goodwill, friendliness, and harmony. It was her against them. She automatically turned people into opponents, and in her mind she had to win every encounter with them.

Barbara drew pleasure and strength from tearing others down. Her act of judging others was aggressive, a way of expressing disdain or diminishing who others were. Although, unconsciously, it felt to her as though she was building herself up by this behavior, actually, the reverse was true. She was placing herself in a basically unsafe position in her relationships.

Needless to say, this took a toll upon her in many ways. She could never let her guard down and lived with a sense of fundamental anxiety and threat. Although she felt that the threat came from others, a deeper reality was that Barbara herself was a threat.

It is said that what we see in others is a projection of how we see ourselves. Relationships are a way of looking into the mirror. The people we attract to us and what we judge or focus on in them are all reflections of who we are as well. That which we cannot tolerate in others is something we have not accepted in ourselves.

Perception Is Fatal

Perception is fatal—it is a selective process and determines not only the people we attract in our lives but the way the relationships will go. What we see in others we actually bring out in them. It is as though we are sending a subliminal message to the person about how we want him or her to be. What we focus upon increases. When you look for, discuss, and dwell upon the faults of others, they will intensify in your life.

This negative way of perceiving must inevitably backfire upon the perceiver as well. By intensely judging (and often damning others), paranoia can develop easily. This is the sense that the world is filled with enemies who are against us in all kinds of ways. In truth, paranoid individuals are really the enemies of others, projecting their own anger upon them. By judging others and seeing the worst in them, they are prevented from realizing the basic fact that it is they who are putting these dark impressions forward and living their lives on the basis of them.

Other Ways We Judge

It may seem as though the mind is wired to measure, approve, reject, and create separation between people. Particularly when we meet someone of a different race, nationality, religion, or culture, our judging minds go into full gear. There is a part of us that wants to be with similar individuals. We feel safer with those we feel similar to, as if we automatically understand them and are standing on the same ground. As soon as individuals who look, act, dress, speak, or think differently from us appear, judgment can become automatic, putting up impenetrable walls.

This phenomenon, which creates prejudice, racism, and all kinds of persecution, is so lethal and automatic that it needs to be looked at carefully. By automatically excluding others from our hearts we cut off wonderful possibilities of encounter, growth, and love.

Do Not Judge
If You Do Not Want to Be Judged

When we indulge in judging others, the other side of the coin is that we feel very vulnerable to being judged ourselves. We become touchy, defensive, and restricted in how we express who we really are and what's going on. We naturally assume that others are judging us, as we are them. This false assumption limits one of the greatest sources of health, happiness, and well-being—natural self-expression. If we fear being judged, how can we spontaneously express that which we truly feel? We cannot, and feelings become backed up, repressed, and ultimately expressed as symptoms of all kinds. By not expressing ourselves, we soon lose touch with what's going on within and can easily become strangers to ourselves as well. The walls around us grow thicker. Soon it's hard to let fresh air and sun in.

Today's Diet

JUDGE EVERYONE FAVORABLY

Because we are so accustomed to judging others, it may be impossible to stop this behavior cold. Instead of even trying to stop it, another way of handling the problem of judging others is simply to turn this malevolent activity around.

STEP 1: *Becoming Aware.*

Without awareness of what we are doing nothing is possible. We start today's exercise by simply becoming aware. Whenever you meet someone today, whether or not you already know the person, become aware of what you are thinking of them—how you are judging the person. Are you looking over what they are wearing? Are you judging how they're standing? Are you making assumptions about what they're thinking? Take a moment to stop focusing upon the person, and become aware of what's going on within.

STEP 2: *Find Something Positive About That Person, Right Now.*

There is something worthwhile about everyone. Find what is good, beautiful, healthy, uplifting, interesting, inspiring, or enjoyable about the person you are with.

Look for it. Focus on it. Appreciate it.

STEP 3: *Acknowledge It to the Person.*

Tell the person you are with what you find positive about him or her. This may be a difficult step for some people to take—they are so used to hiding their good feelings about others and so used to expressing what isn't right. But this step is a crucial one, both for them and for you. Open your mouth and let others know what you appreciate about who they are, how it has impacted upon you.

STEP 4: *Take Time to Take It In.*

Take time to let this sink in with the other person and with yourself. Don't mumble your response and run away. Allow yourself to notice the impact you are making upon the other person, and allow yourself to hear and take in the person's response. Some may offer thanks to you. If so, take it in. Let yourself realize the enormous affect your inner and outer judgments have, not only on others but also on yourself.

STEP 5: *Judge Yourself Favorably as Well.*

Usually those who are busy judging others are also judging themselves harshly as well. This may be done silently and unconsciously, but its effects in one's life are still strong. In this step, we turn that process around. Sit down today, and find that which is positive about yourself. Write it down. Make a list.

STEP 6: *Keep a Book of Praise.*

As you go through the days, keep a little notebook with you and whenever you do something you appreciate, like, or feel good about, take a moment to write it down. This will keep you conscious of the need to focus upon the good not only in others but also in yourself. The more you do this for yourself, the more you will do it for others as well. Read this little notebook once a week. Take it in. Train your mind to refocus over and over again.

Insults
and Gossip

*You add as much strife to the world
when you take offense, as when you give it.*

— KEN KEYES, JR.

LESTER WAS A GOOD-NATURED MAN, usually available to help others and generally calm. His relationship with his wife was stable and nurturing. He was considered a good employee and a good friend. That is why everyone was startled when he blew up at a dinner party after a long-term acquaintance of his casually made a remark about him and his wife that Lester considered insulting.

"Who do you think you are to say something like that?" Lester yelled. "Now I know what you're really thinking. Forget about it—our relationship is over."

"It was just a joke," the friend countered.

But Lester stormed out of the party. The insult had pierced deeply. It hit at a sore spot. The friendship was finished.

Insults

There is nothing more inflammatory, more able to disturb, enrage, depress, and agitate a person than being insulted. It is actually fascinating that a little comment made about a person can cause such turmoil within. Friendships have been lost over it, deals broken, days ruined, and a sense of well-being utterly destroyed. It is crucial to both understand and take charge of this volatile weapon in human life.

What is it about insults that pierce so deeply? And why is it that human beings spend so much time insulting others, either behind their backs or to their faces? (In fact, certain tabloid newspapers can be said to be nothing more than a collection of insults. These tabloids have large readerships. People seem to enjoy hearing insults, slander, and gossip, all of which are forms of one another.)

However, insults are so potentially lethal that in Jewish scripture it is said that if you insult a man in public and shame him so much that it makes his face red, it is equivalent to killing him. What is it that is being killed? The sense of the person's dignity, pride, and well-being. It is an assault upon his soul. And it is an assault that is often hard to answer or to defend against. Insults come suddenly, often when they are not expected. They take a person off guard. They cause him to now distrust the other and the relationship. They stir up the desire for retribution. Also, insults easily spread into other manifestations, such as slander and gossip.

The Effects of Insults

An insult is different from judging someone, because it is done out loud. Usually, we judge others in private. However, when we are insulting someone, it is done in the open, trying to diminish that person's sense of self-worth, causing them to question themselves; when others are present, it causes others to look at this person differently, to interfere with their good opinion.

This practice is considered so dangerous because by insulting others either to their faces or behind their backs you rob them of their good sense of themselves, their good name, and their good reputation. This not only affects their livelihood but can also interfere with their relationships with others. Much pain and serious loss can result, especially when insults develop into gossip and slander.

Gossip and Slander

When we gossip about someone, what we are really doing is engaging in a stream of insults about him or her. We take pleasure in recounting these negative facts and the person we talk to takes pleasure from listening to them. When gossip becomes extreme, public, and persistent, it turns into slander, which is a way of destroying a person.

What is the fascination we have with this kind of activity? When a group of individuals were told that they could not gossip or listen to gossip for a week, they were dumbfounded. "We won't have anything to say, then," they said. "And if we can't listen, we won't be able to participate in any kind of discussion."

Is it truly possible that most of our social engagement revolves around harming another and listening to harm? Are we aware that we are doing this? What kind of benefit can possibly come to us from this activity?

For many it is a relief to hear something negative about someone else. Once again, it makes them feel better about themselves. This is a false sense of self arising, a sense of self that is based upon comparison with others. It is also called ego or pride, and the strengthening of ego within ourselves is no different from drinking straight poison.

The False Sense of Self

It is the false sense of self, or ego, that responds so violently to insults and at the same time loves insulting others. This false sense of self is shaky, as it is not based upon what is real. It is based upon a hall of mirrors—the desire to look a certain way to others, to receive social approval, and to compare oneself favorably in all interactions. As social conditions and reactions are always changing, the ego can never rest. It can never feel ultimately good enough, and so it keeps the person constantly on edge.

When something is said that offends it, the ego bursts out with anger, hurt, and pain, trying to establish its dominance. Our true self is not vulnerable to comments by others. It is unaffected by praise and blame. The true self knows who it is and is secure in its basic goodness, value, and love.

Needless to say, the ego dominates many people's lives. One way for the ego to protect itself from being insulted is to enjoy insulting others. This is the basis of gossip and slander. It is a false way of building the ego up. However, what we do not realize is that engaging in these practices not only harms others but also harms us. We keep ourselves thinking negatively; we keep upset alive within. We allow our minds and hearts to be filled with bitterness. It is impossible for this bitterness not to rebound upon ourselves. Who can live a healthy, happy, fulfilled life when harboring a bitter tongue and bitter heart?

The True Self

The exercises in this book all aim at diminishing the power of the ego and at giving our true selves room to grow. As our true selves are basically strong, they do not need the false strength of anger. As anger diminishes in our lives, the joy, aliveness, health, and creativity we all long for can be expressed fully.

Today's Diet
DON'T GOSSIP OR LISTEN TO GOSSIP ABOUT ANYONE

Today's exercise has two parts. The first part deals with gossip, or insulting others; the second part deals with ways to handle insults that come our way. Once we have done the first part, the second part is easier.

STEP 1: *Don't Gossip About Anyone.*

This may seem truly impossible at first. It isn't impossible, it's just a big change. Tell yourself it is for one day only. Do this one day at a time. Once you make it through the first few days, it becomes so pleasant and delicious to do this that it will become uncomfortable to revert to your old ways.

Even if you are very tempted to say something about someone, don't. Don't gossip about anything; don't talk about someone else's business. When we start with what seems like harmless gossip, it soon turns into something negative. Before long a remark is made that is insulting about that person.

STEP 2: *Try to Find Meaningful and Interesting Things to Talk About.*

We often gossip because we have nothing much to say. Rather than engage in thoughtful, purposeful, interesting conversation, we just dwell upon other people and how their lives are going. Prepare yourself with other topics to discuss. Take time to think about why you are talking to another person at all. Is it to pass the time of day? Is it because you feel lonely? Is it to seem charming and in touch?

Words are powerful. They not only affect the lives of others, they affect how we are seen as well. They create assumptions in the minds of others. All conversation has some kind of outcome. Take time to decide the purpose of your conversations, what kind of outcome you would like to create.

STEP 3: *Don't Listen to Gossip*

For some this is even harder than not gossiping. We are often the recipients of gossip about someone. It may seem unfriendly or rude not to be willing to listen. But gossip cannot go on unless there are two parties. By changing the topic, or intervening with a kind comment about the person being discussed, we can refuse to become involved with this.

Decide ahead of time what you will say or do when you find yourself the recipient of gossip. Don't leave yourself unprepared and unarmed. Prepare a polite response, such as "I don't really like talking about this person." Or just change the topic. Do not respond. Or immediately counter with something positive and change the topic then.

STEP 4: *Refuse to Be Insulted.*

According to the scriptures of many different teachings, when we are insulted we are being given an opportunity to grow, to elevate ourselves, wipe out bad karma, extinguish sins, or learn a great deal about human life itself. Here is a beautiful quote on the subject by the Indian philosopher Shantideva:

> *When someone who I have given a great deal to*
> *And who has been a source of great hope*
> *Betrays and insults me,*
> *May I regard him as a great sacred friend.*

This means that the person who has insulted or betrayed us is a teacher, someone who has come to either help us reduce our ego, balance our transgressions, learn to develop patience and compassion, learn the art of forgiveness, and just to teach us about the very nature of life and relationships.

If you do not perceive an insult as an insult but as a teaching or a gift, how can it hurt you? Then it is not an insult at all.

STEP 5: *Do Not Answer Back to an Insult.*

On a very practical level, if you are insulted, do not reply. Say nothing. Breathe deeply. Give yourself time. So much harm is created by lashing back, escalating a situation, saying things you may not mean. Just go within and experience what you are feeling. Know that it is the ego, the false sense of pride, that is acting up. Do not go along with it.

In scripture it says that if you allow yourself to be insulted and do not make any response, all your sins will be wiped out. Think of the insult as having come to cleanse you. This will take away feelings of anger and revenge and allow you to view it from a different vantage point.

And in fact, if you do not react to the insult with pain or escalate it, then the insult has failed. It has lost its power to hurt you. And beyond that, who is the beneficiary if you are not left with anger and feelings of revenge? Who is the loser if you are left burning within?

Blaming Others

Do not look at the faults of others.
Look at your own deeds,
Done and undone.

— BUDDHA

WE ALL LOVE TO BLAME OTHERS for everything. Our first reaction to a disappointment, fight, loss, or negative experience of any kind is to look around for someone to blame. It's always someone else's fault. It seems as though we need an object upon which to vent our upset and focus the blame.

Tom was the office manager of a small office. Whenever there was difficulty in the office, either with sales, among staff, or with customers, Tom immediately cast the blame. First it was the different members of the sales staff who were to blame, whom he sought to replace. "If we have a new sales force, we'll do better," he told his boss. It didn't happen.

Then Tom decided the cause of the problem lay among those working in-house. He held weekly office meetings in which he castigated everyone. "I thought they were pep talks," he said later on, as people started leaving.

Finally, as the company's revenues kept declining, Tom roundly blamed the economy. "This situation can't be turned around right now," he told his boss. "It's the same everywhere; the entire industry is hurting. It's the economy."

Tom's boss had had enough of him and he was promptly fired.

"Blaming was how I survived," Tom admitted dejectedly when his own day of reckoning came and he met with a career counselor. "I looked everywhere else for the problem. It never occurred to me the situation had anything to do with me."

Somehow Tom seemed to be constitutionally unable to see his own role in the events that were going on. He always looked outside himself and never took a moment to notice the ways in which he was contributing to the situation.

We hear similar stories in many arenas, including relationships (where people blame their partners), health (where doctors are blamed), failure (where fate and destiny can also be blamed), and so forth.

Searching for Causes Outside Ourselves

Many of us have the same way of approaching difficulties as Tom, whether it be in the realm of business, relationships, family, or health. We immediately search for the cause of our problems outside ourselves. We hear people say, "If only I had a different boss/different job/better doctor/more sensitive partner/bigger bank account/jazzier girlfriend/more beautiful body—things would be different. Then I would be happy."

Here is a shocking piece of news. This idea is completely untrue. No matter what changes take place in your life, nothing will be different if you yourself stay the same.

Wherever you go, whomever you meet, you take yourself with you. External changes simply bring temporary relief and alterations. The basic events that take place in your life, the patterns that repeat around you, are the ultimate expressions of who you are. They are manifestations of often-unconscious thoughts, beliefs, behaviors, and tendencies that express themselves in the outside world. Even if you change the scenery of your life, your basic reaction to life continues unchanged.

Take a long moment to absorb this fact. It is crucial. Just truly understanding and acknowledging this can make a huge difference. Most of us do not realize that this seemingly built-in tendency to blame our failures or unhappiness on outside events or people is one of the main causes of the pain, anger, and frustration we experience in life.

Powerlessness and Blame

This tendency to blame others also has another terrible effect. When we blame others, we temporarily feel as though they are wrong and we are right. Self-righteousness develops. In our minds we become unassailable, different, and better than others. No one can get us. We think we are the strong ones and the others are flawed.

The truth is exactly the opposite. When we blame others, we become weak and powerless. We lose our ability to see what is truly going on. Then, it is easy to be blind-sided by events. Many are shocked to lose a relationship or job and say they had no idea it was coming. This is because they were not in touch with the reality of the situation and were often living in a cocoon, refusing to see their part in the situation. Blaming others takes away our ability to be in charge of our lives. Instead of being strong, we become weakened.

Seeing Clearly

Unless we see the reality of a situation clearly, we cannot act appropriately and make corrections that are needed. Some have such a great fear of being wrong or being criticized or judged that they are willing to give up seeing the truth of what's going on and allow a negative pattern in themselves to continue. This is the effect of pride and ego, causing blindness.

Some people feel that if they include themselves in the problem, this means that they have failed. Just the opposite is true. It takes strength to take responsibility and to realize that when something goes wrong, all individuals involved play a part in it. It also takes strength to realize the difference between blame and self-awareness, between punishment and natural correction.

If we can stop blaming others and start taking responsibility, enormous changes are possible in every area of our lives.

Today's Diet
STOP BLAMING OTHERS

It can be truly daunting but also freeing to realize how much we blame others for that which has gone wrong in our lives. Unfortunately, some forms of psychotherapy encourage this activity. Individuals spend a great deal of time dwelling on their past and blaming all sorts of people and events for who they are today. It is one thing to notice what happened, it is another to wallow in blame. Though this may bring temporary relief, the long-range outcome is destructive. The individual becomes unable to marshal all their present forces to live with power and responsibility today. They become unable to learn and utilize the lessons life has presented.

This program offers wonderful antidotes to blame. Try them. You'll love them.

STEP 1: *Make a List of All Those You Blame for What's Going On Now.*

Next to each person's name, write down what you are blaming him or her for, and the effect it is having on your life now. You will be shocked as you do this exercise. You may have had no idea that there were so many people or events you felt were responsible for your difficulties now. Be gentle as you do this. Just make a list. This is for the purpose of getting a bird's-eye view of your own state of mind.

STEP 2: *Take Your Power Back; Become Responsible.*

Each person you blame is holding on to a piece of your personal power and self-respect. Take it back. Right down next to each one how *you* contributed to the situation. What did you get out of the situation? How did you keep it going? What could *you* have done differently? This is not about *blaming* yourself. It's just about seeing clearly what went on. See your role in it. This is called taking responsibility. It is also called growing up.

Taking responsibility for what happened and is happening in your life is one of the most empowering actions anyone can take. When we take responsibility we say, "I had a part in having things as they are and I now have a part in living differently." New choices become available. Our anger quotient is cut tremendously. We become able to look at people and events with new eyes. Remember, responsibility also can be read as "response-ability"—the ability to *respond*, not react.

Right now, try taking responsibility for one event that is troubling to you. This does not mean blaming yourself for it. It means seeing your part in it. Just see it. Notice what difficulty or trouble you may be causing others. Notice how you are keeping a negative situation going. Notice if there are other options you may have. Do this without guilt or self-punishment. Just notice.

STEP 3: *Stop Blaming Them or Yourself.*

Blame involves castigation and condemnation of some kind. Here we simply ask that you try to *see* what happened. Let go of all the anger you have toward others and yourself. Just look clearly. Anger prevents us from seeing the whole picture. Here are some ways to let go of the anger and stop blaming:

1. Make a list of three good things you got out of the situation.
2. Make a list of three ways you grew as a result of what happened.
3. Make a list of three ways in which the person you blame was having a hard time and struggling.
4. Make a list of three ways you could have helped them.
5. Make a list of three ways you would now do things differently.

As we let go of blaming we develop compassion. We also realize that mistakes in life are natural and inevitable. And they are just mistakes. They can be corrected. Mistakes do not mean that there is something terribly wrong with us or others.

Review and Repair

Leave no traces.

— Zen saying

EVERY FIVE DAYS we have a day that is dedicated to "Review and Repair." This will give us a chance to absorb and integrate the most important points from the previous days and to see how they work in conjunction with one another. It will also give us a chance to reflect on what has happened, on how we have reacted to it, and on how others have reacted to us as well.

This day is very important. Usually we keep absorbing new material, but do not take time to stop and truly digest what we have taken in. We do not allow ourselves to feel the effects of what we have absorbed or take time to notice what is needed now.

The "Review and Repair" day is a day of reflection. We take time to look at the events of the past four days. We note the changes we've made and the results of new actions, and get in touch with corrections in our lives that may be needed.

During the normal course of our lives we may notice that repairs are needed in our homes, clothing, diet, activities, or relationships. We notice these in passing and plan to take care of them at some time or other. In this way we leave little trails of messes around.

In this program, time for review, repair, and corrections takes place on an ongoing basis. There is a beautiful Zen saying, "Leave no traces." This means do everything completely. Do not leave a little trail of messes behind you. Pick up your coat and put it where it belongs. Take time to keep your promises. Mend broken fences. Clear away rubbish. Fulfill the words you have spoken.

In this program each of the preceding days has been filled with new ideas and actions. Today we take time to look at the effects of our words, thoughts, and deeds. We see what is now needed. And we do it.

Today's Diet
REVIEW OF THE PAST FOUR DAYS

STEP 1: *The Most Meaningful Ideas*

Write down the most meaningful ideas of the past four days to you. What about them touched you?

STEP 2: *The Most Meaningful Exercises*

Which exercises were most meaningful to you? Why? Would you like to make some adjustments to them? It's fine. Do it. It's wonderful to take what suits you and fine-tune it. We are all different. A little adjustment here or there makes it your own.

STEP 3: *The Most Difficult Exercises*

Which exercises were most difficult? Were there some you could not or would not do? That's fine as well. It's to be expected. It's also extremely valuable to notice which ones they were. Take a little while to reflect upon this. What was it about these exercises that was so difficult or unpleasant to you? Can you see how doing them might make a difference in your life? Would you be willing to try even one of them? Would you be willing to do one today?

STEP 4: *The Most Meaningful Interaction*

As we undertake these exercises, new and meaningful interactions take place. It is inevitable. Write down what happened to you. Describe your meaningful interactions. What else happened between you and others? It's good to keep a record. As we go through this program it will become fascinating to look back and follow the trail we have gone along.

STEP 5: *Changes That Are Needed*

Write what changes you notice are needed in your life as you have gone through these past few days. Don't be afraid to write down anything that you think of. You will not have to do them all at once. Just make a note of them. Simply realizing that changes are needed is a huge step. Most of us don't take time to pay attention to this. Acknowledge yourself for being willing to be aware of changes that may need to take place.

STEP 6: *Actions That Are Needed*

As we do these exercises we can become aware of people we haven't called or contacted, gifts we haven't given, projects we've left unfinished, dreams we've left unfulfilled. It's helpful to write these down. Just make a list. Don't become overwhelmed by it. Just write it down.

STEP 7: *Changes That Have Taken Place*

As we go through these days we will also become aware of natural, spontaneous changes that have taken place in the way we see things and relate to others. Write these down. They're fascinating. Many happen all by themselves.

STEP 8: *Actions That Have Taken Place*

Just as changes have naturally taken place, we most likely have taken many new actions. Keep a record of these. It is very easy for things we do to slip away. If we do not take time to notice and record our actions, they escape our view. The more we notice and become aware of what is going on, the more power it has in our lives and the lives of others. We also receive encouragement and inspiration by taking time to realize and absorb what is happening.

STEP 9: *New Possibilities*

Here is our chance to write down any new steps we may wish to take. Anything can be included, in any area of our lives. As we go through this program, new desires, goals, hopes, and possibilities will be arising. Don't let them slip away. What are the new possibilities that are appearing on your horizon? Write them down. Give them life.

STEP 10: *New Promises*

Do you want to make a promise to yourself today? This is a strong resolution that is important to you. Promises have power. Keeping a promise is even more empowering than making one. Start off by making a promise you can keep. See how it feels to keep it.

STEP 11: *Wins*

Here is the place where you list your gains in well-being. The mind naturally wants to negate change, progress, and new steps. By taking time to review and repair what is going on we turn that process around. We acknowledge what we are doing and what its consequences are in our lives. As you do this, you will be amazed at how many ways you win. What you focus upon increases, and the more you focus upon your wins, not your losses, the more they will appear in your life.

Happy sailing.

Depression

*Human happiness comes
from perfect harmony with others.*

— CHUANG-TZU

IT MAY BE SAID that depression is one of the major illnesses in our country, one that tremendous numbers of people are treated for. The label "depression" is actually used to describe a whole host of conditions ranging from severe psychotic incapacitation to a consistent state of feeling blue. Along this spectrum depression takes many forms and can be triggered in a number of ways, including those that are hormonal in origin.

This chapter is not intended as a review of all the ways in which depression manifests. If a condition is causing difficulty in eating or sleeping or is creating thought disorder or anxiety, which incapacitates, it is certainly necessary for you to obtain proper medical attention. This discussion of depression is based upon a psychological view. It will offer an understanding of the psychodynamics of depression, and ways of handling it when it is not extreme.

The Nature of Depression

Psychologically speaking, depression is often thought of as anger (sometimes rage) that has been turned against the self. In these cases, an individual who is filled with frustration, resentment, and unacknowledged anger has no other way to express his state of mind. The anger therefore becomes turned within and produces a sense of lethargy, hopelessness, bitterness, or despair.

The depressed individual loses a sense of joy and enthusiasm in life. As he projects his state of mind upon the outside world, he sees and expects the worst, often fearing disappointment and loss no matter what he undertakes. Strong cynicism can develop. This negative point of view can further evolve into catastrophic expectations. In this condition, a great deal of fear or anxiety develops as the individual imagines different catastrophes that are about to take place.

Catastrophic Expectations

Needless to say, there is a delicate balance between clear and honest assessment of reality, and worry that escalates into a state of catastrophic expectation. Particularly now, as we deal with the threat of terrorism, this point is crucial to understand. So many are suffering from ongoing depression and anxiety as they are informed about current events. It is one thing to take proper note of difficult conditions, no matter where they may appear, and another to respond with depression and excessive fear. A healthy response is to note what action is needed and take it, and not to dwell upon all kinds of possible consequences that our imaginations can embellish in many ways, many of which never happen. However, when individuals are living with depression, it is easy for them to project their own depression upon external events. This causes the catastrophic expectations to seem more real to them.

In order to be best able to handle that which we are faced with it is necessary to stay focused upon what is real, to become fully present, now. This allows us to respond in a balanced way to actual danger and to simultaneously see how and where one is safe and strong. Then we can easily know appropriate actions to take.

Psychosomatic Illness

Another way in which depression manifests is by causing all kinds of aches, pains, accidents, and chronic illness. The sorrow that an individual lives with and that is neither expressed nor handled can become diverted into physical symptoms of all kinds. This is not to blame the person who is suffering, or to say that the discomfort is unreal. It is only to point out that a generic cause and fuel for psychosomatic illnesses is often found in the depression the individual is suffering from.

When an individual feels helpless to deal with life situations, uncared for, overly pressured, unheard, or misunderstood or feels too alone, these feelings easily become converted into physical illness. These illnesses are then a cry for attention, help, or love. For some, illness becomes the only way in which they can allow themselves to express their need to be dependent, or to ask for the attention, love, and care they are hungering for.

For others, illness becomes a wonderful way to manipulate and control others and demand their needs be met. For some it is the only way they can say "No" to demands made upon them that they cannot meet.

Ongoing illness and pain are often natural ways for hidden depression and anger to be camouflaged and expressed.

Today's Diet
MAKE FRIENDS WITH YOURSELF

The very best antidote to depression is acceptance of yourself. In depression we are covertly attacking ourselves with our anger. In this program we turn that around by overtly making friends with ourselves. Rather than being our own worst enemy, we will become our own best friend. We are like another person to ourselves. We can give ourselves that which we have been wanting from another. We do not have to feel helpless or hopeless thinking there is no way to receive what we need. The very best first step is to begin by giving it to ourselves.

Acceptance is a vast phenomenon. It is the great medicine for most pain. We begin to learn how to give and receive acceptance as we do the exercises.

STEP 1: *Pinpoint Life's Disappointments.*

Write down what you are angry about in your life. It doesn't matter whether or not it seems rational or mature. Just write down what you truly feel. No one will see this. This is a time and place to start truly communicating with yourself. Do not censor or reject what you are feeling. Just write it down. This is a big step in making friends with yourself, to allow yourself to express what is true for you, and not to judge or blame yourself for it.

There is a huge difference between expressing what you feel, becoming aware of it, and acting it out. Depression arises because we do not allow ourselves to even acknowledge the truth of what is going on inside. We judge and censor ourselves. We refuse to accept all of who we are. By finding out what is truly going on with ourselves we are slowly taking off the lock that keeps depression in place.

If you can't say it in words, draw a picture. If you can't draw a picture, get some clay and make a symbol of it. Find some way to begin the process of becoming your own friend, of allowing yourself to feel what you are feeling and allowing yourself to know it. As you accept what you feel, these feelings can then dissolve and change. It is lack of acceptance that holds things in place. It is lack of acceptance that keeps us stuck.

STEP 2: *Make a New Self-Assessment.*
Most of the depression we feel results from thinking ill of ourselves. We blame ourselves for everything. We declare ourselves to be failures, stupid, patsies, or someone whose judgment cannot be trusted. We then feel we should be punished, and most of us know how to do a good job of it. In this manner we disable ourselves, and invite depression and hopelessness.

In this step you begin to create a new self-assessment. Write down the ways in which you blame yourself for your disappointments. What decisions have you made about the person you are? It is these decisions that are keeping you depressed. It is these decisions that are preventing you from growing strong.

Now, stop blaming yourself. Accept what happened. Realize you did all you could at that particular point of your development. Experience giving yourself acceptance, relating to yourself as a good friend would. Acceptance doesn't mean it was right—or wrong. It just was. It happened. By accepting the fact, you will be able to move forward.

Acceptance is a potent form of strength and comfort. Acceptance allows us to begin the process of healing and moving forward, rather than continue to beat ourselves up for what happened. It also allows us to mobilize many hidden resources we have for becoming strong again.

STEP 3: *Discover Inner Resources.*

Each one of us is gifted with inner resources that can enable us to deal with whatever challenge presents itself. Depression covers over these inner resources, telling us that there is no way out. In this step, we turn a deaf ear to the voice of depression, and uncover the inner resources we have.

Find a time in your life when you felt powerful and able to handle whatever came your way. Write down a little paragraph about it. Describe who you were then.

Now, look and see what inner resources were alive at that time that allowed you to handle things as you did. Describe them. Write them down.

Recognize that our natural inner resources never die. They sometimes go undercover, but they can always be called back again. These resources are yours to live with your whole life.

Tap into one inner resource today. Focus on it. Call it to you. Let that inner resource be with you as you go through your day. Let it guide you in new actions and decisions. Use it consciously.

STEP 4: *Declare Your Life Purpose.*

It is impossible to be depressed when we are focused upon a larger purpose. When we are depressed we are basically focused upon ourselves and how our lives are going. When we open our vista and place our attention upon a larger purpose, upon ways in which we can contribute and make a difference to others, depression has no place to take hold. This focus upon a larger purpose and the actions it generates provide energy and aliveness. They produce a sense of well-being.

Think about your larger purpose in life. What did you used to believe it was?

What do you think it can be now? Write down some of your thoughts.

This is a large topic and there are many paths into it. Just to begin exploring our larger purpose is a wonderful antidote to depression. Even though it may be hard to do so, taking little steps in the direction of something meaningful to you shifts the depression and allows light to come in.

Playing the Victim

The ways you think you are,
Not the ways you really are,
Are the bars on your own personal prison.

— Zen saying

UNFORTUNATELY, these days it is quite fashionable to identify oneself as a victim.

There are many organizations that cater to victims of all kinds of abuse, and a variety of individuals wear the label of being a victim as something they are proud of. It provides a sense of justice and perhaps also conveys the idea that these individuals who have been wronged now have a right to be angry, and to seek redress and justice.

This is a complicated issue with many social and legal implications. Here, I would like, however, to simply look at this question of the relationship between victimhood and anger from the point of view of ways to rid oneself of anger and of all the negativity it causes in our lives.

Who Is the Victim?

If we consistently think of ourselves as and call ourselves victims, it is inevitable that we take this identity on. For some, being a victim has an odd kind of power; it gives them permission to be angry, and to continually seek revenge. After a person has been injured, it is very understandable that they may feel weakened and have the wish to gain power back again. The real question is: What is the best way to strengthen and empower this person? Is it useful, empowering, or healthy to continually keep in mind that they have been unfairly injured? The term itself, "victim," implies that the individual had no power or control over what has happened to them. Is this the identity we want to live with? That very notion continually takes away a sense of present strength and responsibility for events in one's life.

There are many victims' advocacy groups whose members wish to balance the scales now. While justice is wonderful and necessary, at what cost do we seek it? Some are willing to maintain their helplessness and anger for long periods of time until they feel the wrong they have suffered has been righted. Others use their sense of victimhood to take out their anger on others. They seem to feel they have a right to hate whole groups of people, or behave in negative ways to others because they were once victims of some kind of terrible abuse. They now feel that they have the right to be depressed, nasty, or unwilling to participate in life. All of these are secondary benefits that victims can sometimes claim.

What does this do to the individual? It does not allow them to move forward. It keeps them bonded to the painful situation. It keeps them filled with hurt and anger. It keeps them viewing large groups of people (one of whom may have been their attacker) in a skewed way. It justifies ill will of all kinds. It closes many doors in their life. They have truly become a victim now—of themselves.

Blaming the Victim

Many are very careful about not placing any responsibility for what happened upon the person who was hurt, on the victim. This is called "blaming the victim."

Some acts of injury are random. Others happen to certain individuals frequently. There is a pattern in the kind of abuse that individuals draw to themselves. It is not "blaming" the individual to point this out. It is respecting the person, by looking at ways in which they may have advertently or inadvertently contributed to what happened. This attitude gives power back to the one who has been harmed. It asks: What are different kinds of ways we can react to what happened? What kind of lessons can we learn? When we are stuck in an identity such as that of victim, there is nowhere to go. The actual identity of "victim" disempowers those who bear it. It implies that there is no real way they can erase the trauma and live a healed life now.

Erasing Trauma

Trauma can be erased. We do not have to live with an event that hurt us unless we choose to do so. If, however, we cling to secondary benefits that we reap from our injury, we may not be so eager to erase the trauma we feel. However, the basic fact of the matter is that the event that harmed us is over now. Yet its effects can go on for years. What keeps these effects alive? What keeps the pain and trauma going? These are crucial questions, because when individuals are in a posttraumatic state (which can go on for many years), they are actually reliving the injury they suffered over and over again. It takes time to realize that they are re-creating it over and over themselves within their own minds.

Some individuals can go through a hard experience, get up, integrate it, and move on. Others cannot. Those in the first group do not hold on to anger and revenge. They have other things in life to focus on. The first group of individuals may have a stronger sense of who they are. The injury has not gone deep enough to make them question their self-worth. The first group of individuals may realize that life presents various blows and may have not personalized what happened. It did not happen because of some great flaw in themselves.

When we understand how truly toxic anger and vengeance are to our systems, we will realize how important it is to give up all kinds of self-imposed identities that keep us angry and upset long after the time we have been harmed.

Today's Diet
GIVE UP BEING A VICTIM

We all play the role of victim at one time or another. For some it is a major identity; for others this role creeps in unconsciously at different occasions. It is never a valuable way to approach our life experience.

STEP 1: *Meet the Victim.*

Take note of the victims in your life. Who are they? Which individuals play this role consistently? Write down their names.

How do you feel about them? Do you enjoy their company? What are they implicitly saying to you? How are you answering?

Now, look at the times and places in which you've played this role yourself. What spurs it on? What benefits do you get from playing the victim? How does it make you feel?

STEP 2: *Letting Go of Victimhood.*

Notice yourself in a situation in which you play the victim. Now, in your mind, let go of that role completely. See how different you feel. See other ways in which you could view and respond to the situation. Practice this in your mind.

When you catch yourself playing this role in life, let it go completely. Do nothing. Be there just as you are. Look at the situation through brand-new, open eyes.

Notice how differently others respond to you. Notice how different you feel about yourself.

STEP 3: *Opening New Possibilities.*

List three things that being a victim prevents you from doing.

List three things you could do if you were not a victim. Do one of them today.

Tomorrow do another.

Remain aware of all the new possibilities that appear as you give up being a victim and reclaim your own strength and power.

Playing the Martyr

*You will never receive more from another
than you are willing to give yourself.*

— Zen saying

MOST MARTYRS do not think of themselves as martyrs. They may describe themselves instead as long-suffering, put-upon, taken advantage of, taken for granted, or unable to say no. These individuals are usually not compensated properly; they are not acknowledged, thanked, or appreciated. They just keep giving, no matter how one responds. Not only do they keep giving, they clearly express the pain and sorrow others cause them by being so thoughtless, selfish, and insensitive. Martyrs do not enter into mutual relationships. Their very identity is bound up in being wronged and hurt. Sometimes martyrs are described as being a few steps away from being a saint.

Anna was in a relationship with Ralph for four years. She paid most of the rent, and did all the cooking, cleaning, and household chores. She asked for very little from him, and whatever she did request was usually turned down. However, that did not change Anna's behavior; she just kept giving relentlessly.

"One of these days," Anna said, "he's going to realize how much I love him, how much I do for him, and how much he's hurting me."

It did not take much for Ralph to realize how much he hurt Anna, though. "Just look at her face," he said. "Nothing I do can make her happy. Whatever I do causes pain. I feel like a rotten bum staying in the relationship, but she does so much for me, I feel so obligated to her, there's no way I can go."

Giving Versus Manipulating

There's a huge difference between giving to someone and manipulating him or her. Manipulation, disguised as giving, is when one gives in order to get something in return, or to make a point. This is not true giving, but giving that hooks others in, often making them feel badly about themselves. It is giving that demands returns. There is a price tag that always goes with it.

It seems as though the martyr keeps giving, but when giving is not mutual, when only one party is giving and is being hurt or drained by it, then this is not true giving at all, but compulsive behavior designed to control. Some martyrs feel that they do not deserve to be treated with respect. They feel that the only way to hold on to a relationship is to give and not receive in return. Other martyrs enjoy the feeling that they are superior to others and will not sink to the level of those they have relationships with. Sooner or later people in relationships with martyrs feel they owe a great deal to the person, and have no idea how to repay it or how to get out of the bind they are in.

Guilt—the Most Lethal Toxin

Emotionally speaking, guilt is a lethal toxin. When people feel guilty they find some way to punish themselves to relieve the guilt feelings. Anyone who causes another to feel guilty is really causing the person to harm him- or herself. Make no mistake, producing guilt in another is a form of attack.

One of the main consequences of being in a relationship with a martyr is feeling guilt. Martyrs thrive on creating guilt in others. They love making others feel both guilty and inadequate. Implicitly they are saying, "Look how wonderful I am, and look how poorly you're treating me. Because I'm so much better than you, I'll stay anyway and accept this abuse."

Individuals, including children, who are in relationships with martyrs suffer a great deal. They often develop poor feelings about themselves. They cannot express any anger or frustration to a martyr either, because that would only hurt the martyr more—and the martyr is suffering so much anyway at their hands. This anger that cannot be expressed bounces back toward the person, causing him to punish himself. None of this is healthy. None of this has to do with true giving and receiving.

The Difference Between Guilt and Healthy Remorse

This step is extremely vital for our mental health. Needless to say, we all make mistakes and either consciously or inadvertently do harm to someone. When this happens, it is necessary to acknowledge what occurred. It is natural to feel badly or remorseful about it. The feeling of remorse, empathy with others, allows us to develop compassion and to grow.

Remorse is not the same thing as feeling guilty, however. Remorse leads to realization; remorse leads to taking action to correct the wrongdoing, and then moving on. We do not stay stuck in remorse for years. We do not wallow in it. We do not use the remorse we feel as an excuse for not doing what is needed to correct the situation, to apologize or find some way to make things right.

Guilt operates differently. When people feel guilty they often wallow in it. They think that the pain of guilt, the self-punishment, is payment or correction for the wrongs they have committed. It isn't. You can feel guilty and downtrodden for years and nothing good comes out of it.

Guilt often reinforces the sense that one is bad, helpless, and unworthy. It disempowers and even cripples people and prevents them from learning from their mistakes and taking new, healthy, corrective action. The mistake or wrongdoing is not the basic issue. The issue is what do we learn from it, how do we grow, how do we become better because of it and make a more significant contribution to the world. Guilt prevents this from happening. Remorse is a healthy first step.

Today's Diet
STOP MAKING OTHERS FEEL GUILTY; STOP TAKING IN GUILT

Today's exercise is both for martyrs and for those in relationships with them. Both are doing this dance together. As soon as one person changes some steps, the dance is done.

STEP 1: *Give Up Your Suffering.*

Both martyrs and those in relationships with them are usually attached to their pain. The martyr is long-suffering and their partner suffers as well, feeling that they have hurt the other and are unworthy. This pain has turned into an identity. It makes a martyr feel victorious that they can stick out the painful situation for so long. There's a sense of strength in being willing and able to endure suffering. A reverse pleasure exists.

The martyr's partner feels they are someone who hurts others and therefore are no good. They can never satisfy their partner nor make them happy, no matter what. Recognize that this is false. There are plenty of people you can make happy and give to if you wanted to. Instead of choosing someone healthy you receive false pleasure and revenge out of holding out on the martyr. But take a moment to recognize the price you pay for this.

- Decide to give up these roles. Stop doing the dance.
- Martyrs: Say no to your partner whenever you want to.
- Those in relationships with martyrs: Start saying yes to everything. Give your partner what they want, including acknowledgment.
- Ask yourself this question: "Who would I be without my suffering?"

Try this and see what happens, to both you and the other person. It's actually easy to break out of these roles as soon as you see that they are not serving you.

STEP 2: *Stop Giving Guilt.*

Because guilt is pure poison, it is a wonderful step to stop giving guilt to others.

Realize that no one else is responsible for your happiness. Don't put your life on someone else's shoulders.

Notice the ways in which you are acting wounded, hurt, wronged, and saddened around others. Stop doing it. Go cold turkey on this. Implicit in this behavior is not only blame of others, but secret demands that others should make your world right. Not only is this impossible, it is the kind of demand that pushes others away. Those who stay and get pulled in by the guilt usually end up feeling trapped. They also feel like failures when they realize that nothing they do can really make you happy and end up secretly resenting both you and the relationship.

STEP 3: *Stop Taking Guilt In.*

Those who are the rescuers, who get pulled into the guilt trips of others, realize that this is a huge trap. You are putting your energy into a bottomless hole. Not only can you not make things right for others, but also you will end up drained and rejected in the long run. And if and when things do go well for the martyrs, they very often get away from the rescuers as soon as possible. They do not want to be reminded of that time in their lives when they needed rescuing.

It's one thing to offer constructive help, direction, and suggestions to others when requested. It's another to feel that a person's entire life is in your hands. It isn't. If you want to believe it is, or run your life that way, take a good hard look at what it is inside of you that thinks it's benefiting from the

rescuer role. Also, take a good hard look at the consequences to you of behaving this way.

STEP 4: *Start Giving and Receiving Appropriately.*
Both martyrs and their partners must learn what true giving
and receiving are.

True giving is when you give for the joy of giving, not
demanding anything in return. Try it at least once today.
Find something you want to give to the person just for the
joy of giving it.

When you receive fully and freely, that too is a gift. True
receiving includes fully accepting someone's gift, enjoying it,
acknowledging its source, and offering thanks. Once this
cycle is complete, there is nothing more to be done. You do
not owe the giver anything. Just by receiving in this manner
you have given a great deal.

Today, take note of what you receive all day long. See
how you receive it. Are you receptive, aware, and thankful
for the gifts given to you? Make a point, today, of receiving
at least one thing freely and fully.

Being Better Than Others

Who is wise? He who learns from everyone.

— PIER KE AVOT, Jewish scripture

MOST HAVE A BUILT-IN NEED to compare themselves to others, to be better, to compete and win in all areas of their lives. They do not realize, however, that this is an expression of aggression toward others, and ultimately also toward themselves. When we want to be better than others, we are also driven to make sure they remain beneath us. We do what we can to keep them in their place, suppress, revile, and deceive them, and we look for their failings and weaknesses. We may also take pleasure in their hardships and losses.

This explains the fascination many have with gossip, slander, and learning about the troubles encountered by people in high places. When famous people fall from their pedestals and suffer, many feel relief that they are not so much better after all. Those who feel pleasure at the hardships of others have been busy comparing themselves and have come out on the low rung.

Maria was so competitive that she could not bear the sight of a younger or prettier woman. The moment one entered her world, either at the office or socially, she immediately felt as though she shriveled up inside.

"I had to get rid of her as soon as possible," Maria admitted. "There wasn't room in this world for both of us to survive."

Maria's response was automatic. She would do all she could to cause the person difficulty. When this happened at the office, she would look for any little thing the woman did wrong and gossip about her to superiors. She made sure that the woman never received the support or information needed to do the job. Maria constantly feared that her job was at stake and not only her job, her sense of pride that she was better than all others and was ultimately irreplaceable.

How We Compare
Ourselves to Others

Although the example of Maria may seem extreme, it is a good example, because many individuals live with a version of her behavior, whether it appears in the arena of sports, family, love, or relationships. Some are not able to relate at all to others who they feel are "better than them." They fill their worlds with those who they feel are inferior—and treat them that way, to keep them in their place. Some are drawn to those whom they experience as better than them, but the essence of the relationship consists in tearing the person down, in subtle and not so subtle ways. Others channel this need through being members of a team and taking great relish in beating the other team, proving that they are "best."

Living this way, one becomes unable to see the beauty and gifts that each person possesses and that they could otherwise share with you. Living this way, one lives in bad faith, being an enemy to life, not a "friend." This way of being keeps the prideful person nervous, tense, on edge, looking for ways they can maintain their imagined superiority. Relationships become power struggles. There is little fulfillment or peace.

Pride Versus Self-Worth

Pride is a sense that I am better than others, I have the ultimate beauty, talent, and answers, and I alone should rule the world. Others should look up to me and realize how privileged they are to be in my presence. I, on the other hand, can dismiss them. Who are they, after all? We recognize this attitude in many so-called gurus, leaders, tyrants, and fanatics. It can take a while to see that there is nothing behind these false claims, except the fierce, destructive energy of pride.

Pride creates a grandiose, false sense of self and causes the prideful person to close themselves off to many situations, possibilities, insights, and relationships because they do not believe others are worthwhile. Pride causes an individual to be out of touch with the reality of who they truly are, of what really brings happiness. Pride prevents a person from experiencing their true value, or the true value of others.

A sense of self-worth, on the other hand, provides equanimity and enjoyment when dealing with all kinds of individuals. When an individual has a true sense of self-worth they do not need to compare themselves to others, to tear others apart or feel superior. Instead there is an experience of oneness and sharing. By recognizing where one's true value lies, one simultaneously recognizes the true value of others. One also recognizes, as Emerson wisely said, that each rose in the garden has its own special beauty. One rose does not compare itself with another. It just blooms as it is intended to bloom.

Today's Diet
STOP BEING BETTER THAN OTHERS

Undoing pride can be a lifelong process, because pride, competitiveness, and comparing ourselves to others has been so deeply ingrained in our lives. However, as soon as we get a real taste of the joys of living without pride, life becomes much simpler. We then can spot pride in the many guises in which it appears.

STEP 1: *Recognize the Many Faces of Pride.*

Because we are so accustomed to pride, the first step is to recognize the many times and places it arises during our day. It is also necessary to recognize our own special brand of pridefulness and how it operates in our lives.

1. Make a list of those to whom you feel superior. Who are they? Why are you better than they are?

2. Make a list of those you feel are better than you. Who are they? How does this make you feel? How do you behave with them?

3. Make a list of those you avoid contact with completely. Why do you avoid them? What do you think of them, and what do you think they think of you?

This exercise will surprise you. It's okay. Be surprised. Be honest with yourself. You may also be astonished to see how many people you've written out of your life.

STEP 2: *Stop Comparing Yourself to Others.*

1. Pick someone on your list to whom you feel superior. Write down all of this person's positive qualities. Now, stop comparing yourself to this person. Let her be who she is. Let you be who you are, as well. Enjoy the differences between the two of you.

2. Do the same with someone you think is better than you. Write down all of your own positive qualities, as well as this person's. Can you allow both of you to have positive

qualities, though they may be different? Can you stop comparing in this case as well?

STEP 3: *Arrange a New Meeting.*

1. Contact a person to whom you feel superior and arrange a meeting. Go out to lunch together, or breakfast, supper, or tea. Pick someone you can actually spend time with.

2. Make the meeting all about the other person. Don't talk much. Listen. Really find out about them. Give them a chance to be the star.

3. Do the same with someone who feels they are better than you. When you give them a chance to be the star and really find out about them, you'll be amazed to discover how much they crave being heard and known, how shaky they are about their true identity, how much they need to be seen and heard. You don't have to tear them down to feel good about yourself. You don't have to agree with their view of you or themselves.

STEP 4: *Each One Is the Best One.*

Take this practice with you in your daily life. As soon as you notice yourself feeling better than another, let it go and let the other be the star. Notice the wall you are placing between yourself and who they truly are. Why are you doing that? There's nothing to hide from. Both of you can be wonderful.

As soon as you notice that you feel someone else is better than you or that they feel that way and are trying to convince you, rather than looking for that individual's failings, just look for the ways in which you two are different. Look for their good qualities and yours as well. Look for what you have to give them, and what they have to give you. Find out more about them. Talk to them about themselves and really listen. Let the true person they are emerge. Don't buy into a fantasy. It won't do you any good.

Review and Repair

Today's Diet
REVIEW OF THE PAST FOUR DAYS

STEP 1: *The Most Meaningful Ideas*

Write down the most meaningful ideas of the past four days to you. What about them touched you?

STEP 2: *The Most Meaningful Exercises*

Which exercises were most meaningful to you? Why? Would you like to make some adjustments to them? It's fine. Do it. It's wonderful to take what suits you and fine-tune it. We are all different. A little adjustment here or there makes it your own.

STEP 3: *The Most Difficult Exercises*

Which exercises were most difficult? Were there some you could not or would not do? That's fine as well. It's to be expected. It's also extremely valuable to notice which ones they were. Take a little while to reflect upon this. What was it about these exercises that was so difficult or unpleasant to

you? Can you see how doing them might make a difference in your life? Would you be willing to try even one of them? Would you be willing to do one today?

STEP 4: *The Most Meaningful Interaction*
As we undertake these exercises, new and meaningful interactions take place. It is inevitable. Write down what happened to you. Describe your meaningful interactions. What else happened between you and others? It's good to keep a record. As we go through this program it will become fascinating to look back and follow the trail we have gone along.

STEP 5: *Changes That Are Needed*
Write what changes you notice are needed in your life as you have gone through these past few days. Don't be afraid to write down anything that you think of. You will not have to do them all at once. Just make a note of them. Simply realizing that changes are needed is a huge step. Most of us don't take time to pay attention to this. Acknowledge yourself for being willing to be aware of changes that may need to take place.

STEP 6: *Actions That Are Needed*
As we do these exercises we can become aware of people we haven't called or contacted, gifts we haven't given, projects we've left unfinished, dreams we've left unfulfilled. It's

helpful to write these down. Just make a list. Don't become overwhelmed by it. Just write it down.

STEP 7: *Changes That Have Taken Place*

As we go through these days we will also become aware of natural, spontaneous changes that have taken place in the way we see things and relate to others. Write these down. They're fascinating. Many happen all by themselves.

STEP 8: *Actions That Have Taken Place*

Just as changes have naturally taken place, we most likely have taken many new actions. Keep a record of these. It is very easy for things we do to slip away. If we do not take time to notice and record our actions, they escape our view. The more we notice and become aware of what is going on, the more power it has in our lives and the lives of others. We also receive encouragement and inspiration by taking time to realize and absorb what is happening.

STEP 9: *New Possibilities*

Here is our chance to write down any new steps we may wish to take. Anything can be included, in any area of our lives. As we go through this program, new desires, goals, hopes, and possibilities will be arising. Don't let them slip away. What are the new possibilities that are appearing on your horizon? Write them down. Give them life.

STEP 10: *New Promises*

Do you want to make a promise to yourself today? This is a strong resolution that is important to you. Promises have power. Keeping a promise is even more empowering than making one. Start off by making a promise you can keep. See how it feels to keep it.

STEP 11: *Wins*

Here is the place where you list your gains in well-being. The mind naturally wants to negate change, progress, and new steps. By taking time to review and repair what is going on we turn that process around. We acknowledge what we are doing and what its consequences are in our lives. As you do this, you will be amazed at how many ways you win. What you focus upon increases, and the more you focus upon your wins, not your losses, the more they will appear in your life.

Happy sailing.

Suspiciousness

Give others the benefit of the doubt.

— CHESBON HA NEFESH

IT IS EASY TO BECOME SUSPICIOUS of others. By now, we have seen that there is a part of our mind that loves twisting and turning our experiences, framing them in the most dark and fearsome way. Just as children love going on scary rides at the amusement park and find a thrill in conquering ghosts and devils, so that part of our mind loves terrifying scenarios whenever it can find them. Some live most of their lives on one roller-coaster ride after another. First they are up high, soaring to the heavens, then they are quickly plummeting toward hell. On their fall to the bottom, suspiciousness often comes into play.

Allen was a wonderful husband, a good employer, and a dear friend. All went well in his life until one day the phone rang. He picked it up and listened. First there was silence, then a male voice scoffed and hung up. At first Allen paid no attention. He went back to what he was doing and decided it was a prank caller. After the call came the second time a few moments later, Allen was rattled.

This wasn't a random call, Allen decided. Something more was involved. In fact, he'd heard that voice before somewhere. Allen sat down and tried to remember where. As he sat there mulling over it, the thought came to Allen that somehow or other this man was involved with his wife.

The snake had whispered into Allen's ear and Allen listened. He took in what the snake had to say. The thought came that his wife was having an affair. That's why she was out later than usual during evening meetings at the PTA, that's why she was exercising and looked so pretty. Allen's peace of mind vanished. He then became prey to nagging doubts about everything. Allen began building a case against his wife, first in his mind, then outwardly. He could not rest. He began tracking her every movement, entering her e-mail, getting her phone records. Everything she did became further proof of her wrongdoing. Finally, Allen hired a private detective.

By then Allen's marriage was over, irrespective of what the detective found or did not find. Allen grew silent, withdrawn, and sullen when his wife was around. Their physical life together ended abruptly as well. Allen even began thinking of having an affair himself, to get back at her, equalize matters, and feel good about himself once again. How dare she do this to him? Who did she think she was?

By the time the detective told Allen that there was absolutely no evidence of any wrongdoing on the part of his wife, Allen was inaccessible. He was totally caught up in his delusion. Some psychiatrists or psychologists might say that Allen was now paranoid.

From Suspiciousness to Paranoia

Although Allen's case may seem extreme, it is actually a wonderful example of the way in which suspiciousness, when it takes root, can quickly grow like a weed, crowding out reason, good sense, fairness, and balance, and can quickly metastasize into strong delusions about what others are doing or have done. The individual who dwells upon these delusions, who has been taken over by suspiciousness, often sees himself as a victim of some kind of secret conspiracy. Needless to say, he reacts with hurt and rage and with plans of his own about how to redress these wrongs.

When these delusions are very strong, reality takes a backseat and what we call paranoia appears. This is the feeling that others are against us, can't be trusted, and are planning evil behind our backs. Many paranoid individuals are very bright and seem to function beautifully. It can be quite a shock to realize that they are living in the midst of these delusions, that they basically distrust the whole world and expect attack in return. It can also be a shock to realize how much time they spend planning ways to protect themselves and get revenge.

Psychologically speaking, Allen was projecting his fear upon his wife, and then behaving as if what he feared was so. The seed of suspiciousness triggered something in him, and a deeper doubt, fear, or insecurity started to grow. Allen lost sight of the distinction between what he was feeling and what was actually happening in the outside world. A paranoid individual projects his own anger and fear upon others. As he fears others and wants to hurt them, he thinks they feel the same way he does.

Suspiciousness and Romantic Relationships

It is not unusual to see this dynamic operating to one degree or another in romantic relationships. In romantic relationships both partners feel vulnerable. They naturally fear losing the partner, or being rejected. It is not unusual to feel insecure about oneself and one's ability to keep the relationship going. However, when suspiciousness really takes root, these individuals then look around for ways to project their fear and insecurity upon their partners. They believe their partners are doing wrong, preferring others, planning to leave. Suspiciousness can then intensify, with many destructive consequences.

Suspiciousness at the Workplace

Needless to say, suspiciousness can become a lethal component at the workplace as well. When the environment is overly competitive, many individuals feel that others want to take their jobs away. They cannot trust anyone. Rather than being able to be part of a team, they have to guard their position. Life becomes each man for himself. The joy of working together is over.

Others fear rival organizations. Some are constantly on the watch for company spies. Some are suspicious of the opposite sex and their true intentions. However and wherever it manifests itself, suspiciousness is a force to be contended with. There is a huge difference between being conscious and aware of natural dangers and lapsing into suspiciousness. Awareness provides neutral and clear information. Suspiciousness destroys trust and goodwill.

Today's Diet
GIVE OTHERS THE BENEFIT OF THE DOUBT

Today's antidote to suspiciousness is extremely effective and beneficial: Give others the benefit of the doubt. To the individual who is in the grip of suspiciousness this may seem like foolishness or leaving oneself unguarded. The opposite is true. It is suspiciousness that takes away one's ability to see situations fully and clearly and that prompts behavior that is destructive. It is the individual who lives with suspiciousness whose life becomes constricted.

STEP 1: *Pinpoint Your Suspiciousness Quotient.*

Many of us do not even realize how suspicious and untrusting we are. We need to stop a moment and see how we are interpreting events. When you feel uneasy, threatened, out of balance, or generally wounded, stop and take time to write down what you feel went wrong. This is an amazing first step. So many are absolutely stunned to realize that they feel others have done them wrong or are planning to do so.

STEP 2: *Undoing Suspicion.*

Put down the name of the person you feel is not on your side. Write down why you feel that way. Make a list of the reasons.

Then, next to each reason that leads you to feel suspicious of the person, write a different interpretation of his or her behavior. Find a different way of interpreting what happened. Find several ways. Here's an example:

Person: Audrey did not call all week.
Interpretation: She is sick of me. Found someone better.
Reinterpretation: Audrey is worried about her sick mother. Possibly spending more time with her. Perhaps busy shopping for supplies her mother can't get on her own.

We do not ever react to what is actually happening, but to our interpretation of it. It is crucial to see the way you habitually interpret events. Some people always interpret things in a way that is personal to them, feeling that someone is actively trying to hurt them. If you tend to react this way, notice it and turn it around.

You may not be able to control what happens, but you can control your interpretation of it. Choose a positive interpretation. Give others the benefit of the doubt. By doing this *you* will be the beneficiary. You will not have to walk around tied up in knots.

STEP 3: *Reality Checking.*

We are certainly not suggesting that you hide from the truth of what's going on by making up favorable interpretations and denying reality. We are simply pointing out that when we automatically choose suspiciousness, we are not necessarily seeing reality either.

This next step of reality checking is central. Rather than cook up ideas in your mind about what's happening, check out the truth. Get in touch with the person whose actions you are concerned about. Set up a meeting. Ask questions. Do it without blame or accusation and suspiciousness. Meet with them to really find out.

This means that you must be open to listening and hearing what the other person says. You must be fully willing to consider the facts as they present them. You may also use this meeting to present them with your own doubts and feelings in a nonthreatening way.

When we speak the truth to others in a neutral manner, it takes the charge out of a situation that is building up. When we communicate about what is bothering us and stop pretending that it isn't, this gives the other individual a chance to come forward and let us know more about himself and his point of view. It also stops games from developing in destructive ways.

STEP 4: *Make New Choices.*

At this point, it is crucial to add that all healthy, life-giving, supportive relationships are built upon mutual trust. After a careful, honest, and fair examination in which you give the individual you're in a relationship with a full opportunity to express their position, you may conclude that the person you are involved with is not trustworthy. It is then appropriate and often beneficial to make new choices for your life.

Being with an untrustworthy person on an ongoing basis keeps you off balance, anxious, and unable to build a relationship upon a foundation that will allow it to thrive. You have a right to make healthy choices for yourself. When you eliminate unnecessary suspiciousness and are able to see clearly, it is possible to see whether a person or situation is right for you. Then your choice of friends is based upon wise discrimination, not delusion.

CHAPTER 17 • *Day 12*

Self-Sabotage

Let your eye look with kindness,
Your tongue speak with sweetness,
And your hand touch with softness.

— SHIVANANDA

SELF-SABOTAGE is actually a strange phenomenon that is very common. It is the action an individual takes, consciously or unconsciously, to harm themselves. At first it seems difficult to understand why an individual would pull the rug out from under their own feet, why they would undertake a project or relationship and, when all is going well, find a way to ruin it. Many individuals who are in the grip of self-sabotage either are unaware of what they are doing or are unable to control it. Some can't figure out why things start off beautifully and in a little while fall apart.

Mark would start out wonderfully at whatever job he undertook. He would move into his new office, set up systems, make new friends, and seem to be on the upswing. He generated sales easily and received positive attention from both his colleagues and his boss.

But after around six months of this positive behavior, Mark would begin to feel anxious. Initially he would experience the anxiety as restlessness, telling his wife he was getting bored with the job. He would also frequently find something wrong with the way others at work were performing. Soon he would start staying out after work, either drinking with friends or taking in a movie. When Mark began coming home later and later his wife didn't know what was going on. Naturally, she suspected a girlfriend. Now his marriage became rocky as well.

Before long Mark didn't return calls promptly at work and stopped doing the follow-up he used to do so well. As his performance on the job declined, Mark found many people and reasons to blame it on. When his wife pointedly asked how he contributed to the mess, Mark had no idea what she was talking about. In fact, Mark was in the grip of self-sabotage.

Fear of Success

There are many factors that contribute to self-sabotage. Fear of success is a prominent one. Although they do not realize it, many individuals will not allow themselves or their projects or relationships to succeed. Some feel that they do not deserve it. They harbor guilt or shame about who they are and will not allow themselves to win or to have that which they want in life.

Some have a long history of being told by parents, friends, or teachers that they are not worth much. Some have told it to themselves. Like a poison arrow, this negative barb has gone deep within. These individuals, believing it is true, cannot allow themselves to shine.

Some feel that success itself is dangerous: The more successful they are, the happier and more fulfilled they are, the more others will dislike them. They subconsciously fear the jealousy of others and the negative repercussions that may come their way if others envy them. Others fear success because they will feel guilty about having more than others have.

Still others get a reverse pleasure out of failing. They refuse to give their wives or family the pleasure of seeing them succeed. They are punishing others by failing, not wanting them to reap the fruits of their success.

Attacking the Self

Needless to say, when an individual cannot express his anger and frustration outwardly, when he cannot even allow himself to have angry feelings, this anger often turns around and becomes expressed against himself. Individuals attack themselves in many ways, and are usually unaware when this self-sabotage is happening.

Some ways of attacking the self include consistently choosing the wrong person for a relationship, choosing a job that is not right for you, staying in negative situations that pull you down, being with people who do not respect you, taking on projects or challenges you are not suited to handle, unhealthy eating and exercise patterns, poor hygiene, or refraining from finding appropriate medical care. Some people begin acting out in ways that causes them to be rejected. Others secretly know just what to do to upset others. Some run away at the last minute, renege on promises, or can't be counted on.

Passive-Aggressive Behavior

A wonderful way of sabotaging relationships is through passive-aggressive behavior. This is behavior that makes a person look good, calm, and centered on the outside, and makes the other person look like they are the bad one, always complaining, angry, and upset.

A passive-aggressive individual, rather than owning and expressing their anger and feelings appropriately, express their anger by what they "do not do." They withdraw, they deprive the other, they refuse to do what is asked for, or they'll do it much later on.

A passive-aggressive husband will either pretend he hasn't heard what's asked of him or offer to do it later, after the need passes. The partner is put in the position of having to beg, nag, or remind him over and over. He then blames his wife for his not doing what is needed because she is such a nag and always upset. He does not see that he has stimulated her upset passively, by his lack of response.

Passive-aggressive behavior is a wonderful way to sabotage not only others but oneself. These individuals often see themselves as put upon by others and as having no responsibility for the situation they're in. In fact, they are sabotaging everything by not taking responsibility for their behavior or their feelings.

Addictions

We could devote an entire chapter to addictions, but many books have been written on this subject. In the context of self-sabotage, addictions are a primary way in which individuals sabotage their lives.

Addiction to alcohol, drugs, gambling, work, sex, love, or whatever form the addiction takes is a powerful way to destroy health, joy, and success. Individuals lose control not only over their addiction but also over the direction of their entire lives. Their focus, energy, time, and money all go toward the substance they crave. This craving prevents them from seeing the many facets of reality or participating in life in a healthy, fulfilling way.

The question of how one gets hooked into addictions is complex. Often it starts as a retreat from life—a way to get some pleasure. Soon it takes the individual into a world of its own, where they can escape facing difficult issues.

That which started as pleasure turns into poison. At first an addiction seems to give something; soon it takes everything away. It is crucial to realize that by giving in to an addiction, by not going for real help, the person is actually aligning themselves with that which does them harm.

Today's Diet
TAKE WONDERFUL CARE OF YOURSELF

Many need permission to take good care of themselves. Some feel it is selfish or indulgent. They can take care of everybody else, but not themselves. Others feel that they do not deserve this good care, or that it is a waste of time. Whatever your excuse for not looking after yourself, today you'll begin turning that around.

STEP 1: *Self-Sabotage and You*

We all need to take a moment and see the subtle, and perhaps not so subtle, ways in which we sabotage ourselves.

1. Make a list of things that do not go well in your life—repeatedly.
2. What seems to go wrong?
3. How do you contribute to that? What do you do? Or not do?
4. What are other ways you could respond? List a few.

STEP 2: *Giving Yourself What You Need*

1. In each situation that goes wrong, what do you need to make it go right? Make a list.

2. Today give yourself one of the things you need. Tomorrow give yourself another.

3. What do you need in general that you presently feel you are not getting?

4. Give that to yourself as well. One day at a time.

STEP 3: *Communicating Honestly*

Believe it or not, one of the best antidotes for self-sabotage is open and honest communication, both with others and with yourself. When we give ourselves permission to express our anger or upset responsibly, we do not have to take it out on either others or ourselves.

1. In a situation in which you see yourself sabotaging yourself, see what it is you are not saying to someone about that situation. Say this responsibly. This means do not blame, attack, or accuse the other. Simply say, "This is how I feel about _____. You are taking responsibility for how you feel, not projecting it upon someone else.

2. Then, ask for what you need to make things better. You will be amazed at how many people have no idea what it is you need in a given situation. When you ask for what you need (and give the other person room to say no), suddenly new worlds open before you. You realize that

it is possible to get your needs met. You do not have to attack either yourself or another.

Step 4: Make Friends with Yourself—Part 1
Making friends with yourself is so vital to well-being that it will be discussed in a variety of ways as we go through the book. There are many exercises that contribute to this process. Let us start one now.

1. Write down what is it that you want in a good friend. Make a list of the qualities.
2. Give this to yourself. Each day choose one item on the list and give it to yourself.

When we learn how to become our own good friend, we develop the ability to stop self-sabotage before it starts. And we have that which we long for from others with us wherever we go.

Low Self-Esteem

*Everyone can be great
Because everyone can serve.*

— Martin Luther King, Jr.

Many individuals suffer from what is commonly called "low self-esteem." This includes feelings of inadequacy, shyness, lack of confidence, shame, and generally feeling badly about oneself. Some will even be surprised to see low self-esteem included as a form of anger. It seems as if low self-esteem is a realistic assessment that arises from comparing oneself to others, from projects undertaken that have failed, or from the many criticisms or scoldings one has received. Others mistake low self-esteem for humility. The two are not the same. True humility is healthy and life-giving. Low self-esteem is not.

Rachel could never win with herself, no matter how hard she tried. Even when she succeeded at various projects, rather than take the success in and feel good about herself, she always focused instead on what she did wrong. She then blew it up out of all proportion. She dwelled upon ways she could have done better. Before long she felt disgusted with herself, calling herself a fool for not seeing in advance what could have been done.

This behavior went on at work as well as in her relationships. Rachel constantly tried harder and harder to do better. She felt so bad about herself she felt it was inevitable a boyfriend would leave her unless she gave relentlessly. Much as she expected, her partners did leave. No one likes to be with someone with such low self-esteem.

Needless to say, Rachel's perspective was skewed. She lost sight of the full picture, both at work and in her relationships. All she could see were her failings. It's quite easy to realize that Rachel's low self-esteem only permitted her to see that which was "bad" about herself, and insisted that she punish herself by reviewing her failings constantly.

How Low Self-Esteem Develops

If we take a moment to consider it carefully *we are like another person to ourselves.* We can be kind or cruel to ourselves. We can praise or vilify. We can keep ourselves up at night, tormented by negative thoughts, or soothe and praise ourselves, adjusting our perspective, finding and dwelling upon that which is positive, and healing ourselves. Basically, although it may not seem so, the choice is up to us.

There is a part of ourselves that watches our own behavior, thoughts, and wishes and judges relentlessly. It decides what we are and are not worthy of, what we can and cannot do. This part can be a tyrant. It enjoys the negativity it puts forth and often keeps up a running commentary within, constantly chastising, complaining, or finding fault. Although we may be sweet and kind on the outside, so often we are certainly not sweet and kind to ourselves within. So many are their own worst enemies, unable to win in their own eyes. Paul Tillich, the great theologian, has described it this way: "We live under a power that seeks to crush us." That power is the part of us that generates low self-esteem.

Low Self-Esteem and Submissiveness

There are many ways in which low self-esteem infects our lives and directs our actions. An individual with low self-esteem can become overly submissive. As they believe they are worthless and that their views, hopes, and dreams do not matter, they often seek someone who is powerful, in control, often authoritative, and do as they are instructed. Behaving this way, they often lose touch with who they really are and their own abilities and resources.

They fear losing the relationship if they are not submissive, and do not realize they are losing themselves. These individuals often become dependent personalities, looking for an infusion of strength and wisdom from outside themselves. Unfortunately, the people they are depending upon often can and do take advantage of them, causing their self-esteem to drop even lower.

Low Self-Esteem and Feelings of Hopelessness

Low self-esteem naturally gives rise to hopelessness. Some say that a feeling of hopelessness is part of depression, but if we look closely, we can see that it is a direct outgrowth of low self-esteem. When an individual feels hopeless about their own life, or about the world they live in, they feel helpless, as though they are powerless to do anything to make changes. They feel hopeless and helpless because they feel they do not have strength, direction, or meaning in their life. This is because they are continually discounting whatever it is they feel and believe. They have twisted themselves to please others for so long, they are out of touch with their own core values. They have also forgotten that each individual on this earth has something of great meaning to share. It is their low self-esteem that is causing them to wipe themselves out.

Today's Diet
GIVE UP NEGATIVE THOUGHTS ABOUT YOURSELF

Today's exercises are so important that they may be said to be foundational.

Unless we can rid ourselves of negative thoughts about ourselves, we will find it difficult to experience permanent health, success, joy in relationships, or gratitude toward life. Once we validate and acknowledge our own resources, all kinds of new possibilities become available to us.

STEP 1: *Low Self-Esteem Is a Lie.*

It is crucial to recognize that low self-esteem is a lie. Despite the mistakes we have made in our lives, each individual is valuable. Most of the ways in which we judge ourselves are built upon lies we have accepted as truths.

List three ways in which you lie to yourself when you think negatively about who you are. Write down each lie, and ask yourself, "Is this really true?" Dwell upon it. Would you judge another person that way for this reason? Is it true that you are irremediable? Do you really deserve the punishment you give yourself?

STEP 2: *How Your Low Self-Esteem Operates.*

Just by becoming aware of the ways in which your own self-esteem operates, you will have begun the process of undoing it. As soon as we bring light, or awareness, into this dark corner, low self-esteem melts away.

Write down what it is that you so dislike or disrespect about yourself. Just make a list.

Write down the negative talk that goes on within. What do you say to yourself about this? We all usually have an inner dialogue that goes on and on keeping these painful thoughts going. Write yours down.

How do these thoughts and words affect your behavior? How does your low self-esteem impair your quality of life? What would you do if you didn't have it that you're not doing today?

STEP 3: *Turning Low Self-Esteem Around.*

1. Write down what you like and respect about yourself. Don't take "Nothing" for an answer. Keep sitting there until you find something to add to your list. The more you do this, the more positive traits you will find.

2. Turn the negative talk around. Consciously write and speak some positive statements about yourself. Say them out loud. Say them in the mirror. Look at yourself and start the process of seeing what is valuable about your life and saying it so. Do this once a day—for example, in the morning as you brush your teeth.

3. Find one thing that you are not doing due to low self-esteem, and do it today.

For some this step may be very difficult. So start with something small. Perhaps you can give yourself a little free time to take a walk in the park? Perhaps you'll buy a magazine you like and read it? As your self-esteem muscles grow, the actions you take will develop into bigger steps of being able to express and enjoy who you really are.

STEP 4: *Building Your Self-Esteem Muscles.*

The more we do these exercises, the stronger we will grow. When we work out in the gym we sometimes become achy. We can feel a few aches and pains here as well. Tolerate them if they arise. They are simply growing pains for your life.

1. Make a list of actions you would do if you felt good about who you are (group A).

2. Make a list of actions you would stop doing if your self-esteem were high (group B).

Do one action on your list from group A, and stop one from group B. Do this until you are comfortable with it. Then go on to the next action on your lists. Start simply and keep going. It is the perseverance that counts here. Just keep going, no matter how it makes you feel. Before you realize, these actions will become natural to you. The negativity will be dissolving. A new you will be born.

Deception

Nothing is hidden.
Since ancient times,
It is all clear as daylight.

— Zen saying

So MUCH HURT and pain arise from our feeling of having been betrayed. Not only does this experience undercut the foundation of our relationships with others, but it can cause us to lose trust in ourselves. We blame ourselves for having been deceived, for not being smart enough or mature enough to realize what has been going on. Deceit rips the fabric of good faith in our lives. Many who have felt betrayed by spouses or people in authority in their churches, schools, or families lose their ability to respect not only those individuals but all that they are associated with. They generalize that all of the individuals in that organization are deceitful. The organization does not stand for anything good.

Great bitterness results from deception, and not only bitterness, but also a sense of meaninglessness in life and difficulty moving on. Trust has been violated. We do not want this to ever happen again. Now we do not know what to put our faith in.

Kamella was a trusting wife and raised her children with a full heart. When her husband began staying out later and later after work, at first she simply attributed it to increasing business demands. When his absences extended over weekends, she used the time to take the children and visit the family. Even when he began receiving phone calls at home, late at night, she found reasonable explanations for it. Finally, after six months of this, a girlfriend of hers who said she couldn't bear to see Kamella being made a fool of took her out to lunch and told her that her husband was having an affair. Kamella sat there in shock.

"I'm stupid," she finally uttered.

"Not stupid," her friend said. "Too trusting."

This painful story went on and on until that family broke up. The important point here, however, is that the deception caused Kamella to lose trust not only in her husband but in men, marriage, and relationships and ultimately in herself. It took a long while to repair this.

Forms of Deception

Deception comes in many forms and disguises. Cheating in relationships is one of the most common and most lethal. Many are on the alert for this. However, there are other forms of deception, also lethal, that we all engage in or are on the receiving end of. Little white lies are common and don't seem to mean much to people. They fib, exaggerate, and spin tales naturally, as if it were expected.

Games, pretenses, and casual promises not kept also deceive others. Even though commonplace, they are still attacks upon another person's trust. When we play games, we are not what we are representing. Whether or not we realize it, we are creating confusion and a lack of balance. Although we may not think they mean much, these forms of deception become habitual and accumulate. When they are part of our daily lives, they become a silent poison infiltrating our lives, taking away our health and fulfillment.

Hypocrisy

A hypocritical person says one thing and does another. He pretends to be someone he is not. Either through dress, actions, words, or conversation, the hypocritical person is in the process of deluding you and also himself. Some hypocrites are so lost, they have truly forgotten who they are. When hypocrisy goes to the extreme, we see con men or women, sociopaths who routinely pull the wool over the eyes of others to get what they personally need and want. They usually want honor, acclaim, wealth, or stature that is not their due. In fact, they are seeking to steal it from others, without truly meriting what they receive.

Beware of hypocrites. Beware of being hypocritical as well.

Lying

There are many ways in which we lie to ourselves and others. It is so important to become clear about this because lying causes us to forget who we truly are, what we are here for, and how to find joy and meaning in our lives. As we lie, we build a wall of fantasy that we become trapped in. We lose sense of our direction and of what is really happening moment by moment. As we lose touch with basic truthfulness, more lies or delusions develop. These begin to seem real. The danger escalates, both to us and others.

Lying includes not simply saying untruths but also exaggeration, communicating mixed messages, and implying things you do not mean. Lying includes nonverbal communication—acting one way when you feel another. It includes the unwillingness to communicate—shutting yourself off. You are lying to another by withholding the truth of who you are.

When we minimize, dismiss, deny, and pretend something isn't happening we are also engaged in lying. Often we lie to ourselves.

It takes great strength and courage to look at what is before us, to see it as it is, and go on from there. As we grow able to do this, lies and the need to lie fade away.

Stealing

Stealing is another form of deception that is all too common. Stealing, taking that which is not yours, is a direct form of deception and attack. It is an assault upon the person you are robbing. It is necessary to realize that one can steal a lot more than personal goods.

We can also steal another's time, energy, pity, focus, relationships, friendships, and enthusiasm. We can take away or steal a person's good opinion of him- or herself. We can steal their hope and joy in life. Theft takes many forms. A hypocrite steals the respect or admiration of others. Many people are thieves and do not know it. Many others are stolen from every day. This is important to realize. We have to stop both.

Today's Diet
STOP LYING—LIVE THE TRUTH

Many of us fear that the truth will destroy us. Actually, the opposite is true. It is the lies we tell ourselves and others, deception in all forms, that weaken and unravel what could be a beautiful life.

STEP 1: *Give Up a Lie a Day—Go Cold Turkey.*

If you get in touch with the ways you live with lies in your life and go cold turkey for one day, you will be amazed at how good it will feel.

1. Write down all the lies you tell yourself and others.
2. Next to each lie, write down what purpose it serves.
3. Next to each lie, also write the effects it has upon you— and the one you lie to.
4. Go cold turkey. Just for today. Cut it all out. Just stop it.

You may have to become quiet. You may have to stop old patterns. Remember, it's just for today. As you do this, you will begin to notice the way others are also lying to you. Do not judge them. Just notice what's happening. Notice how we're all caught in this web of deception. See how it feels to stop it. Take a deep breath.

STEP 2: *Honest Self-Expression.*

When someone asks you something, instead of answering the same old way, take a moment and look within. See how you really feel about the issue. Give them an honest answer. (This does not mean to dump on them, or abuse them. It simply means to take responsibility for how you truly feel and say it. Say it simply. Don't make a big deal about it. Just be truthful to yourself and to them.)

Give the person time to respond. Get quiet and make a space for them to offer an honest response to you. Take it in. Don't fight it. Find out how they really feel.

STEP 3: *Return Something That Is Not Yours—Give Up Stealing.*

Decide what you have taken from someone that was not given, and is not yours to keep. Make a list. Include anything you can think of, not just objects or money.

Return that which you have taken to the person it belongs to. Find a way to do this that you can live with. When you have taken away one's good feelings about themselves, or hope, this can be returned in many ways—a note about how valuable they are, some kind of encouragement. Look within and see all the ways you can make these corrections.

Be aware when you are taking something that is not yours or is not freely given. Stop doing it. Be aware when you are creating a negative atmosphere or feeling in another. Stop this as well.

STEP 4: *Honesty Journal.*

This book is just for you. No one has to see it. In it you will keep track of the lies that you habitually tell to others and yourself, the ways in which you deceive or steal, and the ways you are being honest about the lies and thefts now. Do this daily. Even a line or two makes a difference. Write down what happens to you and others when you give up a lie and replace it with truth.

You may love this so much that you will get addicted to it. This is a wonderful addiction to have. Before long it can replace others.

Review and Repair

Today's Diet
REVIEW OF THE PAST FOUR DAYS

STEP 1: *The Most Meaningful Ideas*

Write down the most meaningful ideas of the past four days to you. What about them touched you?

STEP 2: *The Most Meaningful Exercises*

Which exercises were most meaningful to you? Why? Would you like to make some adjustments to them? It's fine. Do it. It's wonderful to take what suits you and fine-tune it. We are all different. A little adjustment here or there makes it your own.

STEP 3: *The Most Difficult Exercises*

Which exercises were most difficult? Were there some you could not or would not do? That's fine as well. It's to be expected. It's also extremely valuable to notice which ones they were. Take a little while to reflect upon this. What was it about these exercises that was so difficult or unpleasant to

you? Can you see how doing them might make a difference in your life? Would you be willing to try even one of them? Would you be willing to do one today?

STEP 4: *The Most Meaningful Interaction*

As we undertake these exercises, new and meaningful interactions take place. It is inevitable. Write down what happened to you. Describe your meaningful interactions. What else happened between you and others? It's good to keep a record. As we go through this program it will become fascinating to look back and follow the trail we have gone along.

STEP 5: *Changes That Are Needed*

Write what changes you notice are needed in your life as you have gone through these past few days. Don't be afraid to write down anything that you think of. You will not have to do them all at once. Just make a note of them. Simply realizing that changes are needed is a huge step. Most of us don't take time to pay attention to this. Acknowledge yourself for being willing to be aware of changes that may need to take place.

STEP 6: *Actions That Are Needed*

As we do these exercises we can become aware of people we haven't called or contacted, gifts we haven't given, projects we've left unfinished, dreams we've left unfulfilled. It's

helpful to write these down. Just make a list. Don't become overwhelmed by it. Just write it down.

STEP 7: *Changes That Have Taken Place*

As we go through these days we will also become aware of natural, spontaneous changes that have taken place in the way we see things and relate to others. Write these down. They're fascinating. Many happen all by themselves.

STEP 8: *Actions That Have Taken Place*

Just as changes have naturally taken place, we most likely have taken many new actions. Keep a record of these. It is very easy for things we do to slip away. If we do not take time to notice and record our actions, they escape our view. The more we notice and become aware of what is going on, the more power it has in our lives and the lives of others. We also receive encouragement and inspiration by taking time to realize and absorb what is happening.

STEP 9: *New Possibilities*

Here is our chance to write down any new steps we may wish to take. Anything can be included, in any area of our lives. As we go through this program, new desires, goals, hopes, and possibilities will be arising. Don't let them slip away. What are the new possibilities that are appearing on your horizon? Write them down. Give them life.

STEP 10: *New Promises*

Do you want to make a promise to yourself today? This is a strong resolution that is important to you. Promises have power. Keeping a promise is even more empowering than making one. Start off by making a promise you can keep. See how it feels to keep it.

STEP 11: *Wins*

Here is the place where you list your gains in well-being. The mind naturally wants to negate change, progress, and new steps. By taking time to review and repair what is going on we turn that process around. We acknowledge what we are doing and what its consequences are in our lives. As you do this, you will be amazed at how many ways you win. What you focus upon increases, and the more you focus upon your wins, not your losses, the more they will appear in your life.

Happy sailing.

Control and Domination

Of all things, the most yielding can overcome the most hard.

— LAO-TZU

WHEN LIFE PRESENTS MANY CHALLENGES, upsets, and possibilities, the desire to control can seem natural. Many have the illusion that if we control events, ourselves, and others, we will be safe, successful, and secure. Unfortunately, the opposite is true. The more we tighten our grip, hold on, and manipulate, the more out of control we become.

The wish to control arises especially strongly in relationships where people feel vulnerable, where emotions are high, and where a great deal is at stake. At first this may appear as possessiveness, wanting to know all about what the partner is doing, dictating what he or she can or cannot do. Possessiveness often intensifies. Power struggles erupt. There is the sense that the person belongs to you and you have the right to direct their choices and the way their life goes.

Both the person dominating and the one being dominated lose freedom and well-being. Although the dominant ones may say they are doing it out of love, for the good of their partners, the bottom line is that the desire to control is a manifestation of fear and anger.

Love always honors and respects another; it gives a person space to be who they are, to make their own changes and discoveries. It does not seek to take over another's life, but to enhance it.

However, some very much enjoy being controlled. They feel that if their partners are possessive and controlling, it means that they care. This is a dangerous confusion. When one individual controls another, it is always for their own benefit, to make themselves feel safe and secure.

Tara was in a relationship with Robert for over a year before she realized that the gates of her freedom were being shut tight. At first there were only sporadic questions about what went on at work, whom she spoke to, and whom she was with when she stopped after hours into a bar for a few drinks with colleagues. Before long, these questions grew more intense and invasive. Robert wanted her back home at a certain time. If she was late, he became angry. Not only was his insecurity growing, but with it his need to control all her actions and time.

Robert said he did this because he loved her so much; he wanted her with him every moment. At first Tara was flattered. Later on, she felt more and more suffocated and afraid to go places without his permission, more worried about what would happen if she returned a few minutes late.

The Dynamics of Control

The more out of control one really is, the more the desire to control arises. Being able to control another person or situation can provide a feeling of power, strength, authority, or the sense that one's world will stay stable and secure. However, the more we control, the more we crush that which we are controlling, and the more of our own energy we have to use to keep this vigil up.

Control and domination can become an addiction. There is a rush that goes with control—the person feels powerful, as though they are strong and on top of the world. Needless to say, if an individual is addicted to this, he needs more and more of it to keep his good feelings going. Before long he becomes a tyrant, controlling everything in sight.

Sooner or later, all of this has to collapse. Sooner or later, the controlling person has to face that fact that underneath he feels weak and unlovable. He may also feel lost in a world that seems chaotic and uncontrollable.

Fear of Domination

Another strong source of the desire to control others is fear of domination. We do not want to be controlled. We do not want others to dictate our lives to us. Although many long for approval and acceptance, they also fear being dominated by those they want approval from. One way this conflict is handled is by dominating others. They feel that if they are doing the controlling, no one can lasso them in. In fact, they are lassoing themselves, tying themselves to the ones they so need to control.

The Longing for Security

The desire to be secure and feel that our world is stable is deeply embedded in human beings. We will do almost anything to achieve this. The need to control then arises from this. Much anguish, anxiety, and depression can be traced to not having a true sense of stability within ourselves. This happens when we do not live from our own core. When we live a life based upon ego, or upon counting on our money, relationships, beauty, or possessions to provide the security we desire, this kind of life sooner or later lets us down. It is vitally necessary to contact our true source of security, that which provides stability no matter what is going on.

Today's Diet
LET EVERYTHING BE AS IT IS—LET GO OF CONTROL

Today's exercise is extremely enjoyable and rewarding, much more than one might imagine at first. As you do it, you will see how much energy is restored to you, how many inner and outer knots are undone, and how a true sense of inner security grows.

STEP 1: *Think About Whom You Are Controlling.*

1. Make a list of everyone you are controlling—or want to control.
2. Include yourself in this list. Write down the ways in which you control and dominate yourself and others.
3. Think about what the result has been of all this controlling. Have you succeeded in controlling them, despite all your efforts? How has it made you feel? What price have you paid for this?

STEP 2: *Stop Controlling These People.*

Choose one person on the list and just let them be totally as they are. Accept them completely. How does this make you feel now? What happens to your relationship? What happens to your own energy and sense of well-being?

STEP 3: *Granting Freedom to Yourself as Well.*

Now do this exercise with yourself. Allow yourself to be exactly as you are. Stop fighting, pushing, and punishing yourself for the ways in which you function. Take the noose off your own neck.

How do you feel? What new ways of being may be open to you now? What has your endless desire to control yourself stopped from happening?

STEP 4: *Realizing Who Is in Control.*

The purpose of the exercise is to find an answer to this question of who is in control. Different people will come to different conclusions about this part of the exercise. That's fine. Spend time with it. Dwell upon the question of who is really in control of your life and the life of others. Let the answer reveal itself.

1. Who is really in control of this world? Think about that.

2. After you've done all you can, who is in control of what happens to you?

3. What good does it do you to fight life? Is there another way to respond?

Revenge

Do all that is good, refrain from harming.

— BUDDHA

ALTHOUGH THIS MAY SEEM like a difficult topic, let's all pause a moment and realize that much of everyone's life is affected by the desire for revenge. When we have been hurt, betrayed, insulted, or outraged, usually our immediate response is to want to balance the scales, get even, get justice, see the person in pain, cut them out of our life, prove ourselves right, prove that we have been the wronged one. We are the good one; they are bad. We now have the right to get revenge.

Revenge takes many forms; in the most extreme cases it is an individual plotting an outright assault on someone who has wronged them. There are also legal means to do this, such as lawsuits, letters of complaint, and other formal actions. If the wronged person doesn't take immediate action, they begin to stew about what has happened and secretly plot and plan ways to get back at the offender. They stay on the lookout for a chance to get even.

Sometimes revenge takes a quiet and smoldering form—giving the cold shoulder, not answering the phone, gossiping about the person, interfering with his relationships, making sure a person is not invited to a party or doesn't get a promotion at work that he deserves. It may be possible to cause a person to lose his job entirely.

However it manifests, the desire for revenge is lethal and takes its toll more upon the person who wants it than upon the one who has done the wrong. Generally we do not stop to ask *why* we have been wronged in the first place. It may be easy and gratifying to blame the other person, even to see her as entirely bad. It takes a great deal of maturity, courage, and wisdom to step back and look at the entire situation from a much larger point of view.

Henry's wife left him unexpectedly. Although she had told him many times that she was unhappy and had asked him to spend time with her working on changes they needed to make, Henry didn't pay much attention. All women like to complain, he figured. There's no pleasing them.

From his own point of view, Henry did all he could for his wife. He considered himself a model husband. He worked hard, gave her all the money to manage, just kept a little for himself. Henry didn't stray, didn't spend much time with his friends, came right home after work, kept his word, and was on time. He was good to their only son, Jason, too, played ball with him all weekend long. His wife's endless requests for intimacy were confusing to him. She wanted more time alone, affection, romance. Storybook stuff, Henry thought.

When Henry woke up one morning to find his wife gone, he was not only shocked, he was enraged. "You can't please any of them," he kept saying to himself. He felt he'd been weak with her and that's why she'd taken off. Well, he wasn't going to be weak anymore. Right then and there, Henry started plotting his revenge.

Revenge and Helplessness

Basically, Henry felt as though he'd been made a fool of. He felt weak and helpless after his wife left. To him, and to many others, revenge is a way of getting strength back, taking control, showing the world that they aren't a patsy. In their minds they are telling the person, "I'm stronger than you, I'll show you who's boss. I'll do to you what you did to me. Then we'll see who has won."

Nobody wins a game of revenge. Revenge is not a demonstration of strength. It always comes out of weakness, out of a sense of being helpless and having no other way to gain one's honor back again. The feeling that anger is strength is what keeps it going. Actually, anger is an automatic knee-jerk reaction that is born of hurt, helplessness, and loss. Taking revenge is never constructive. Revenge never really addresses what has gone wrong. It drags the person who wants revenge down. It takes his or her joy in life away.

Addiction to Revenge

Once the desire for revenge takes hold, it often becomes an obsession or addiction. Thoughts of getting back at the person take up more and more time in a person's life. Other interests are diminished. The person's life narrows. To a person caught up in this addiction, it seems as though nothing else is meaningful. Life is put on the back burner until they figure a way to get the scales balanced.

We often see this in cases of murder, where the families cannot begin the process of healing until they see the murderer brought to justice. Until that time they are obsessed by the thought of what happened to their loved one and how it must be paid for, the revenge they have a right to get.

Displacement: Taking Revenge on Everybody

Another terrible consequence of the hunger for revenge is that the grievance begins to become displaced, from the one who did you harm to many others. For example, if an individual has been harmed by a person of different color, soon he begins to see all people of that race as culpable. Revenge is taken on anyone of that group, regardless of who they are or the fact that they have nothing to do with the injury.

Revenge is blind. Not only does it cause blindness in the one wanting revenge, but revenge often attacks innocent individuals. When Henry started dating again, about a year after his marriage ended, he received a visceral pleasure from leading on the women he dated. He enjoyed being secretly nasty to them. He would make promises he didn't keep, lie to them, quietly date others simultaneously, do all the things he really wanted to do to his wife now. Henry had decided he was never going to be made a fool of again.

This went on for a long while. Henry's wife was happy in another relationship, and Henry was still consumed with anger. And the women he now dated were bearing the brunt of it. His revenge had become displaced upon women in general. Unfortunately, Henry's story is not so unusual. We see it in many men and women.

The Desire for Revenge and Mental Illness

A major component and cause of mental illness (and physical illness as well) is the desire for revenge. The smoldering anger that is constantly nursed is pure poison. Rather than allow this poison to be released from the system, the person keeps it alive within. The individual who wants revenge has made a kind of vow to himself never to forget what happened, never to let it happen again. He vows to stay on the alert for new possibilities of being wounded and also on the alert for the chance to strike back.

This kind of anger and resentment prevents people from trusting, playing, loving, opening their hearts, or living from the well of creativity within. It stops them from seeing and utilizing their many resources, and building a new life that is stronger and more meaningful because of what happened to them. Holding on to a need for revenge keeps people stuck in the situation that has hurt them, never letting them forget it, never allowing fresh air into their lives.

Today's Diet

FORGIVE EVERYBODY—INCLUDING YOURSELF

The Process of Forgiveness

Most of the exercises in the book up to now are forms of forgiveness. Today we will begin to deal with forgiveness directly. This word has been greatly used and misused. There is a great deal of resistance to it because the process of forgiveness is not truly understood.

Some think that to forgive means to allow an individual to behave any old way, then give them a free pass and go on taking abuse. Others think that all that is needed is to say, "I forgive you," and the pain of the event and the hurt that goes on after it occurred will naturally subside. This is usually not true. So many say, "I have forgiven, but still feel awful."

STEP 1: *What Is Forgiveness?*

Forgiveness is a process. Usually it takes time (sometimes not). There are steps to take, and if we take them in good-will, at some point, when it is ready, forgiveness will inevitably take place all by itself. We will know that forgiveness has happened because we will feel free inside, as if a burden has been lifted. We will feel more alive, healthy, optimistic. We will like ourselves better. We will feel ready to move on.

The first step in the process of forgiveness is to take a look and see how you think of forgiveness, how it functions in your life.

1. What does forgiveness mean to you? Write it down.
2. What are the consequences of forgiveness, as you see it? Write it down.
3. Think of a time in the past when you forgave someone. What happened to you when you forgave the person?

STEP 2: *Who Needs to Be Forgiven?*

Who needs to be forgiven in your life? On whom do you want to take revenge? Toward whom are you holding secret resentment?

1. Make a list of all the people. You may be amazed to see how long this list is. Write it down anyway. As soon as the process of forgiveness starts working in your life, the list will naturally dwindle.

2. Write down what the person did that they need forgiveness for. Be brief and be specific. Don't make a whole story of it. It is the story that keeps the pain of this going.

3. Write down next to every person what you want from them that would help you forgive them. What has to happen to make this situation forgivable? If you say nothing, that's okay. Write it down. If you see the person as totally irredeemable, write it down. Be honest here. And notice also how feeling that way affects you and your life.

STEP 3: *What Do You Need to Be Forgiven For?*

This is a step we usually like to leave out. We usually see the other person as totally wrong and to blame. We seldom want to take a look at how we, too, need forgiveness, or at how we might have contributed to the situation, either knowingly or unknowingly.

Some people focus on how others have wronged them as a way of hiding from this question. It is a defense against looking at what they themselves have done. When a painful situation takes place it is always between two people. Although it may seem difficult to do this step, it is very empowering to see what your part may have been. This is not blaming the victim. This is not about blame at all. It is just about looking and seeing the ways in which we get caught up in a dance.

1. Write down what you need to be forgiven for.
2. Who has to forgive you?
3. Have you apologized or asked for forgiveness?
4. Have you forgiven yourself? What is needed for you to be able to forgive yourself?

STEP 4: *Reconciliation.*

This step is the beginning of healing, which I like to call reconciliation. For some individuals, just doing this step will cause them to let go of their desire for revenge. They will see something, have a moment of acceptance or compassion, or receive a larger view. This step is not about generating guilt, but wisdom. It is about opening up our vistas.

1. For each person who has wronged you, write down three ways your actions may have contributed to what took place. For example, Henry could write down that he refused to listen to his wife or take her requests seriously.
2. Write down what you could have done differently.
3. Write down three ways this person gave to you or served you in the past.
4. Write down three positive traits of this person.
5. Write down three ways this person has suffered and struggled, what difficulties he or she has had to overcome.
6. Write down three ways you have grown strong from this situation.
7. Write down three things you have learned from what went wrong between you and this person.

8. Write down what will happen in your life if you allow this anger to go on indefinitely.

9. Stop writing. Stop hating. See the other person happy and well.

10. See yourself happy and well.

STEP 5: *Tonglen: Send Light and Love.*

There is a beautiful Tonglen practice, which is part of Tibetan Buddhism. The second part of this exercise is to send light and love to others, to feelings, to situations, and to yourself. In the first part, we breathe in the pain or difficult situation; we don't run from it but accept what it is. In the second part, we breathe out light and love. We need not be actually feeling that emotion as we do the exercise. We simply focus on the person, situation, or emotion and say, "I send you light and love." Do it over and over again. This is the most powerful exercise possible. Even a little bit of love heals so much. We have enough love deep within to heal the entire planet, only we are so stingy, we refuse to give it.

Turn that around now. You have nothing to lose but your sorrow.

Abusive Relationships

Our readiness to hurt one another is the meaning
of the separation of life from life.

— Paul Tillich

This topic is a continuation of our chapter on revenge and intimately connected with it. All abusive relationships are based upon the wish for revenge. Although an individual now harms or abuses his partner, coworker, or friend, the desire for revenge has a deeper source. It usually has its source in something (or many things) that have happened in the past. The current person being abused, who is usually dependent upon the abuser in some way, is the tip of the iceberg. The abuser now finally has someone upon whom to get revenge. The sad part of abusive relationships is that the abuser usually harms someone who has given him trust and love.

Unfortunately, there are many ways in which individuals get caught and stay in abusive relationships, not even realizing that is what is going on. Often abusive relationships are similar to the way they were treated as children. They therefore feel comfortable with this familiar treatment. Because they were treated that way as children, some individuals mistake being punished, controlled, and shamed with being loved. They may have heard their parents say when punishing them, "I'm only doing this to you because I love you." Now they connect being loved and being abused.

Andrew felt as though he had to do whatever his boss wanted. He fulfilled all his boss's requests fully and then even did a little bit extra. More than anything, Andrew longed to be approved of and secure in the relationship. He felt that the more he gave, the better his chances would be of being valued.

When his boss realized how deep Andrew's need was for acceptance, he began giving him extra projects to do, having him stay later at work, even having him run personal errands for him. Andrew, who was unable to set appropriate boundaries, wasn't able to say no. At first he didn't even realize that many of his boss's demands were inappropriate.

Andrew began to feel uneasy when he noticed his boss starting to complain about him. Nothing Andrew did was suitable. No matter how hard Andrew tried, the boss found a way to diminish both his efforts and accomplishments. Soon the boss began insulting Andrew in front of others and even yelling at him.

Needless to say, Andrew was involved in an abusive relationship and didn't know how to work his way out of it.

His strong desire for the job and for the approval kept him from responding appropriately.

Different Forms of Abuse

There are many forms that abuse can take. Very often abuse starts out minimally, and often escalates in time. Some forms of abuse include constant criticism, shaming another in public, making demands that are inappropriate and that another cannot fulfill, becoming controlling and possessive, and accusing the other of performing actions that are hurting you. Abuse includes the unwillingness to listen to others, mocking them, and refusing to fulfill appropriate needs in the relationship. It can include flirting openly with others in public or other ways of making a partner feel insecure.

An individual who is being abused in a relationship will notice a great loss of self-esteem. They will begin to feel unattractive, worthless, stupid, or inadequate in some way. When one stays for too long in an abusive relationship, it can be difficult to reclaim one's center again.

Attachment to Abuse

Unfortunately, some people become addicted to abusive relationships. They leave one and go to another. Their low self-esteem, their self-hate, draws this kind of punishment to them. In fact, many individuals become greatly attached to the abuse. This need for abuse becomes expressed personally or even sexually. Without being abused this person doesn't feel cared about or doesn't feel aroused. In professional terminology this has been called masochism, or the deriving of pleasure from being hurt.

Some feel it means they are strong if they can endure in an abusive relationship. They enjoy seeing just how much pain they can tolerate. They have the idea that enduring pain strengthens you, or perhaps cleanses you of your sins. There are many ways of justifying the pain and abuse we are suffering.

Individuals who are trapped in abusive relationships attract it to themselves in other ways as well. These individuals often have a firm investment in seeing members of the opposite sex as hurtful, nasty, or cruel. If this is their image of others, this is what they will attract, and this is what they will respond to in others as well. These individuals often say that kind partners are boring to them. If they find individuals who are kind, they dismiss them as not worth their time. This is because the challenge is gone, and because they are deeply unwilling to see anything good in members of the opposite sex. They would rather hold on to their negative image of others than be happy in their own lives.

Fear of Happiness

Some seek and dwell in abusive relationships because they feel it is all they deserve. It is painful to them to be treated beautifully, perhaps because they did not see their own parents treating each other that way, or perhaps they are carrying deep-seated guilt. Some fear being happy because if they were truly happy with someone and then lost the relationship, the pain of loss would be too much.

Many individuals feel that it is sinful to be too happy. It is better to suffer like everyone else. They fear that if they were too happy, other bad things would happen to them. When we look at this deeply, it seems clear that all human beings feel they must deserve to receive the blessing of love and happiness.

Today's Diet
REJECT ABUSE OF ALL KINDS— BUILD YOUR SELF-WORTH

The process of building one's self-worth is the same as rejecting abuse of all kinds. When we have low self-worth we often do not even realize that we are being abused. By realizing that we are in an abusive situation we can begin to take steps to get out of it and break the pattern in our lives.

STEP 1: *Examining the Relationship.*

Take a relationship you are in that feels destructive to you, in which you feel harmed or diminished continually.

1. Write down what happens in the relationship that doesn't feel good to you.
2. Don't justify it. Just write it down. We have a right to let ourselves know what does and does not feel good.

STEP 2: *What Feels Healthy to You?*

Many of us do not give ourselves a chance to really focus on what would feel healthy and uplifting in a relationship, what it is we really want. Instead we focus upon what we do not like and try to make it end (or endure it). By stopping to take time to notice what we really want, we are beginning the process of re-building. We are allowing ourselves to be really clear about what we do not want. We are also giving ourselves permission to carve out a life that is good.

1. Write down the way in which you would like it to be in a relationship. What feels healthy to you?
2. When have you experienced a healthy relationship? Dwell upon that for a little while.
3. Now, write down what needs to happen for the relationship you are in to be healthy for you. Even if you feel it is impossible, write this down anyway. It will help you clarify who you are, what you need, and what is really going on now.

STEP 3: *Choose to Take Good Care of Yourself.*

It is possible to choose health. It is possible to find the support, guidance, and strength to leave a situation that is harmful. This is a big world. There are many people and possibilities in it. Open your mind.

1. Make a promise to yourself to take good care of yourself.
2. Begin to take good care of yourself in as many ways as you can now (ways that may be independent of the relationship). Exercise, eat healthy, meet with friends, join a workshop, go for a hike.
3. Plan a few healthy, self-constructive activities a few times a week.

This helps you realize that you are not dependent upon your partner for all the attention and care you need. Start giving it to yourself. Start surrounding yourself with others who can give it to you as well.

STEP 4: *Effective Communication*

1. Tell your partner about what it is you need and want. Effective communication with an abusive partner does not include whining, crying, blaming, or making demands. It means sitting up straight and calmly letting the person know what behavior is and is not acceptable to you. Whether or not he or she agrees is irrelevant. You know what behavior you can and cannot tolerate.

2. Set boundaries and keep them. Effective communication also includes setting boundaries. Each human being has a right to set boundaries, to set standards for their own life. If your partner will not keep them or ridicules them, it is irrelevant. It only means he or she is not the right one for you.

STEP 5: *When the Time Comes to Leave.*

If things are not workable and the abuse continues, the only recourse is to leave.

Leave with dignity. Let the person know that you are leaving and why. There is no need to blame or be blamed. Do not get pulled in by tantrums, criticism, or begging you to stay. It is one thing for the abuser to make many promises to be different; it is another for them to truly take responsibility for their behavior and seek the help they need to diligently make changes. Unless they are doing this, it is most likely the abuse will go on and on.

Leaving an abusive relationship not only helps you, it helps the abuser. It is a wake-up call. You are not permitting another person to behave in a destructive, negative manner toward you. You are letting them know there are consequences and that sooner or later they have to stop lashing out and face the problem that resides within.

Dealing with Enemies

Love your enemy.

— The New Testament

MANY PEOPLE'S LIVES center around their enemies. These enemies are considered to be dangerous to them; they threaten their well-being, safety, and security. In order to protect themselves, their entire lives can consist of strategies to beat their enemies, or at the very least to keep them at bay. Rather than living a life based upon a vision of what they want and value, these individuals build their lives around the ways in which they can defend themselves from real or imagined enemies. Their main objective in life becomes being safe.

By focusing so much upon their enemies, these individuals become afraid to take risks, try new activities, meet new people, learn, grow, and develop in new and different ways. Their lives are not about expanding, but keeping things in place. In one way or another, there is always a sense of danger lurking. Even when danger is not really present, just the slightest hint of trouble can easily become blown up out of all proportion.

After years of dating, Tammy finally met Peter, a man she truly cared for. He was attractive, intelligent, successful, and, in her mother's words, a real catch. At first she was tremendously happy with him. Tammy proudly told her friends about the relationship, and gave thanks for it every day.

As time went on and the two of them grew more comfortable together, Peter began to resume some of his old habits—he would stay late after work a night or two during the week. This was innocent enjoyment for Peter; he enjoyed going out with friends from the office for a couple of drinks. Of course, Tammy was not included. No other girlfriends or spouses were. At other times, when Peter and Tammy were at parties together, as was his habit, he spent some time talking to other women there. Peter was naturally gregarious and he thought nothing of this. However, Tammy became alarmed. Before long she felt that Peter was flirting and that ultimately she wasn't good enough for him.

Whereas Peter was once the love of her life he now slowly began to seem more like her enemy. Tammy began to believe that he wanted to take her self-esteem away, make her feel badly about herself. Day after day she grew more insecure. Not only was he her enemy, so were his colleagues at work and all the other women who wanted to steal him from her. Tammy's insecurity began projecting enemies everywhere.

The process of fearing and seeing enemies everywhere can easily grow into paranoia. Before long, no one can be trusted. One has to constantly be on guard. The ability to love, give, and trust becomes damaged. Even when one thinks they are winning over their enemies, they are losing. They are losing a life of freedom, health, and goodwill.

Who Is the Enemy?

We all think the enemy is somewhere out there. There is some person, force, illness, or nation that wishes us ill and is out to harm us in some way. For many people life itself is an enemy, first giving what they desire and then taking it away. Others consider illness or old age to be that which they must battle. For others, death is the final enemy, taking away their very lives.

It is crucial to pinpoint what and whom we consider to be enemies, and how we believe they are going to harm us. We need to see the ways in which this belief affects us, how we defend ourselves, and how we cut off our own life force.

Dealing with the Enemy

It is common sense to believe that we must fight our enemies. We have to outsmart, dismantle, kill, deceive, or betray them and defend ourselves from their attacks. Wars are fought because of enemies, blood is shed, children orphaned, marriages ended, lovers destroyed. The peace in our lives and the lives of others is shattered because of this strong belief.

It is necessary to stop for a moment and take a look at all the actions we must engage in to be safe when enemies appear. What does it do to *us* to have to take these actions? What kind of thoughts, feelings, and deeds fill our days? Is there any way we can live free of anger when our lives and thoughts are obsessed with seeing and defeating enemies?

Enemies consume our time, attention, resources, well-being, and happiness in life itself. And beyond all that, the odd thing about enemies is that even when we defeat one, ten more seem to immediately appear.

It seems there is something innate in the human that enjoys having an enemy. We enjoy conquering danger and darkness. We enjoy feeling that life is a huge battle and that we must always be ready to strike. This builds ego and a sense of power. If I can defeat my enemies, then I am stronger, smarter, or wiser than them. This means I am the better person. This means I can have control over my life. But does it really? Even if you win every battle, do you have control over your enemy or does the need to fight and win have control over you?

How to Get Rid of Enemies Easily

An old saying goes, "Keep your friends close, but keep your enemies closer."

The smartest, simplest, and easiest way to get rid of your enemy is to turn him or her into a friend. It actually takes only a moment to do this. Stop for a moment and ask yourself, "Who decided this person or situation is my enemy?" You did. Now you can turn that decision around and decide the person is a friend. You can decide to become a friend to that person or situation or condition. You can decide simply to stop fighting and to respond with kindness and care. You can choose to see other aspects of that person that are not in opposition to you. Once you step out of the dance the two of you are doing, how can they hurt you?

The True Enemy in Your Life

The next step, if you were ready, would be to take a deep breath and realize where the true enemy is hiding. What exactly is it that is keeping you in constant turmoil?

What is it that is really destroying your life? What is the best way to defuse it?

This is the moment to realize that your true enemy is within. It is the hatred, anger, fear, and upset that keeps you churning. The true enemy is the propensity we have for projecting our anger and fear outside ourselves and onto the world, for pinning it on people and situations and then battling with them. Until and unless we get rid of anger, fear, and dark fantasies, more and more enemies will keep appearing. Ultimately, they are the creations of our own minds and hearts.

Today's Diet
MAKE FRIENDS WITH YOUR ENEMY

Although today's exercise may seem impossible at first glance, actually it is one of the easiest to do. All it takes is willingness. You must allow yourself a moment of willingness to put down your sword and consider the possibility that your enemy is not that different from you. Your enemy wants the same things in life and is, most likely, just as afraid of you as you are of them.

STEP 1: *Daily Reminder.*

Say to yourself, "Like me, my enemy wants to be happy and safe. Like me, my enemy has suffered and wants to be free of pain. Like me, my enemy is lonely. Like me, my enemy will one day face loss and death."

STEP 2: *Who Is Your Enemy?*

1. Make a list of those people (or situations) you feel are your enemies. You may be astonished to note that even those you love are fearful to you.
2. Write down three valuable qualities this enemy has.
3. Write down three ways you have gained from knowing them.
4. Write down three ways you have at one time hurt your enemy.

5. Write down what is needed for you to see this person as a friend.

STEP 3: *Eat the Shadow.*

The shadow, according to Robert Bly, a well-known psychologist, is darkness within ourselves that we cannot accept or acknowledge and that we then project onto a person outside of ourselves. This other person now seems to contain all the bad that really resides within us. Robert Bly suggests that we "eat the shadow." This means that we should reabsorb the projection, take it back, claim responsibility for the darkness we see in another that we contain as well.

This may be a startling thought to some, but give it some time to sink in. When we truly see how this process works, it is extremely uplifting and strengthening.

1. Upon whom have you projected most negativity?
2. What about this person is so unacceptable?
3. Can you see these qualities in yourself as well?
4. For just a moment, can you accept these qualities in yourself? This doesn't mean act upon them; just accept them for what they are now.

As soon as we are able to see and accept some of our own darkness, we do not have to project and fight it in the outside world. When we see that darkness also exists inside of us, there is the real possibility of dissolving it. We do not have to find someone to carry our darkness for us, or divide the world up into good and evil. We see that we all contain everything, and it is possible to truly heal.

STEP 4: *Reclaim Your Power.*

It is extremely disempowering to project one's darkness upon someone else. It gives the other person power over us. We fear they can harm us. We worry that they are dangerous and possibly stronger. It is far more empowering to be willing to feel and face what is going on within than to waste our energy fighting windmills.

Another benefit of reclaiming our own power is that now we are able to see the truth about others. We can see our common humanity and needs. We can find solutions to the conflicts between us. We can start the very beautiful and healing process of becoming friends.

1. Reclaim your power. See that which is mutual between you and your enemy; see how you are alike.
2. Offer your enemy the gift of respect. Offer your enemy the gift of really listening and knowing them.
3. Stop judging your enemy. Let them be who they are.
4. Give your enemy what they want and need. Just one time.
5. Do it again now.
6. Notice how wonderful it feels.

STEP 5: *Where Is the Enemy Now?*

1. Write down the differences between you and your enemy.
2. Write down the similarities.
3. Take time to notice how it feels to live in a world of friends.

Review and Repair

Today's Diet
REVIEW OF THE PAST FOUR DAYS

STEP 1: *The Most Meaningful Ideas*

Write down the most meaningful ideas of the past four days to you. What about them touched you?

STEP 2: *The Most Meaningful Exercises*

Which exercises were most meaningful to you? Why? Would you like to make some adjustments to them? It's fine. Do it. It's wonderful to take what suits you and fine-tune it. We are all different. A little adjustment here or there makes it your own.

STEP 3: *The Most Difficult Exercises*

Which exercises were most difficult? Were there some you could not or would not do? That's fine as well. It's to be expected. It's also extremely valuable to notice which ones they were. Take a little while to reflect upon this. What was it about these exercises that was so difficult or unpleasant to

you? Can you see how doing them might make a difference in your life? Would you be willing to try even one of them? Would you be willing to do one today?

STEP 4: *The Most Meaningful Interaction*
As we undertake these exercises, new and meaningful interactions take place. It is inevitable. Write down what happened to you. Describe your meaningful interactions. What else happened between you and others? It's good to keep a record. As we go through this program it will become fascinating to look back and follow the trail we have gone along.

STEP 5: *Changes That Are Needed*
Write what changes you notice are needed in your life as you have gone through these past few days. Don't be afraid to write down anything that you think of. You will not have to do them all at once. Just make a note of them. Simply realizing that changes are needed is a huge step. Most of us don't take time to pay attention to this. Acknowledge yourself for being willing to be aware of changes that may need to take place.

STEP 6: *Actions That Are Needed*
As we do these exercises we can become aware of people we haven't called or contacted, gifts we haven't given, projects we've left unfinished, dreams we've left unfulfilled. It's

helpful to write these down. Just make a list. Don't become overwhelmed by it. Just write it down.

STEP 7: *Changes That Have Taken Place*

As we go through these days we will also become aware of natural, spontaneous changes that have taken place in the way we see things and relate to others. Write these down. They're fascinating. Many happen all by themselves.

STEP 8: *Actions That Have Taken Place*

Just as changes have naturally taken place, we most likely have taken many new actions. Keep a record of these. It is very easy for things we do to slip away. If we do not take time to notice and record our actions, they escape our view. The more we notice and become aware of what is going on, the more power it has in our lives and the lives of others. We also receive encouragement and inspiration by taking time to realize and absorb what is happening.

STEP 9: *New Possibilities*

Here is our chance to write down any new steps we may wish to take. Anything can be included, in any area of our lives. As we go through this program, new desires, goals, hopes, and possibilities will be arising. Don't let them slip away. What are the new possibilities that are appearing on your horizon? Write them down. Give them life.

STEP 10: *New Promises*

Do you want to make a promise to yourself today? This is a strong resolution that is important to you. Promises have power. Keeping a promise is even more empowering than making one. Start off by making a promise you can keep. See how it feels to keep it.

STEP 11: *Wins*

Here is the place where you list your gains in well-being. The mind naturally wants to negate change, progress, and new steps. By taking time to review and repair what is going on we turn that process around. We acknowledge what we are doing and what its consequences are in our lives. As you do this, you will be amazed at how many ways you win. What you focus upon increases, and the more you focus upon your wins, not your losses, the more they will appear in your life.

Happy sailing.

Anger in the Family

All mankind is one family, one people.

— MOHAMMED

THE FAMILY is the most common place for anger to erupt. It is also the place where the seeds of anger are sowed. When we live closely with others, when we are bonded to them, attached, dependent, or vulnerable, these individuals have the power to deeply affect our minds and hearts. In these relationships our defenses are more permeable, and our expectations and demands greater.

Images of the Family

We have strong images of how parents, siblings, or children "should" behave. We feel we have the right to demand love and attention from those in the family. Parents have strong feelings that they have the right to loyalty and obedience, just because of their roles—no matter how they actually treat their children. Children often feel the same. There is a common craving for a "happy family," where everyone loves and cares for each

185

other, and where everyone accepts all of one another's difficulties. Unfortunately, this craving is often unfulfilled. For the most part the myth of a happy family is often a dream.

Families are often hotbeds of misunderstanding, resentment, sibling rivalry, jealousy, inappropriate expectations and demands, and lack of acceptance. In fact, families are really fine places to work through many issues and learn how to individuate, grow, love, and accept both others and ourselves.

Clea was in therapy for years complaining bitterly about her mother. Her mother was weak, passive, helpless, and unable to stand up to Clea's father, who abused not only her but the entire family. Her mother spent her time shopping and at the beauty parlor, living a life of vanity, in Clea's opinion. Clea could not and would not forgive her mother for that. She blamed her mother relentlessly for every failing she had. She blamed her mother for the fact that she herself couldn't keep a boyfriend interested and thought she'd never marry. It was her mother's fault, Clea insisted, because she never gave her a role model of how a woman should behave. Clea refused to act like her mother and therefore said she didn't know who she was.

In truth, the mother was not the culprit here, but the smoldering anger that Clea held on to was what was holding Clea back. It was her refusal to accept her mother as she was and realize that Clea had many other role models of women she could identify with. It was her inability to get over her profound disappointment about not having the mother of her dreams. We all hold on to an image of how our parents and childhood should be. When this image is not fulfilled, the anger and disappointment can prevent us from growing up and establishing the life and family that best express our values and vision today.

Identity and the Family

A major factor that contributes to difficulties in families and the emergence of anger is the tendency each member has to identify with the other. There is an implicit idea here that each person in the family reflects the other. Parents feel that children are a reflection of them. Parents also project their worst fears about themselves onto their children, or want their children to make up for errors and disappointments in their own lives. Members of families naturally assume that others in the family are the same as them and that the same kind of life or accomplishments will make them happy. This is a huge mistake, which leads to a great deal of pain. It is interesting to notice how little room there is for differences in most families. Most think that a perfect family is one in which everyone is the same, or where parents can provide role models that children wish to grow into.

Individuation— Becoming Who You Are

The most vital process that goes on in the family is the process of individuation. This means that as a child grows, or as married couples live together over the years, they are given the opportunity to discover who they are, to be separate and different from those they love. Some cannot bear this. They experience differences between themselves and family members as separation, or even rejection. They do not realize that unless family members become who they are—individuate fully—they will not be able to love fully. Instead, anger, deep resentment, and pain develop. We see this most keenly during adolescence, when young people are in the process of establishing a new identity and when the process of rebellion against family views and values is most intense. However, at this stage, and all stages, the greatest longing most family members have is being known, heard, and accepted for who they are. Ultimately, this is experienced as love.

Unfulfilled Needs in the Family

After a certain point of maturity family members enter the larger world and become part of other groups. These new groups are often experienced as new families. Needless to say, these individuals automatically and unconsciously begin to repeat the same patterns they experienced in the family they came from. If there were many unfulfilled needs in their original family, they try to get these filled now. If there were many demands made upon them, they expect that to be true once again and begin resisting demands made on them in their new groups. Or they may turn it around and make those demands upon others now. When they enter a romantic relationship, often it becomes a repeat of the relationship they saw between their parents, or a relationship in opposition to it. One way or the other, the original family remains the main reference point.

Conflicts, demands, and unfulfilled needs must fundamentally be traced back to their origin in the family and resolved there. Sooner or later we must make peace with our family, as it was and as it wasn't. Then we become able to create something healing and new.

Families of Choice

When we have come to peace with our family, we are then able to choose those individuals and relationships that we value and want in our lives. Although we cannot choose our original family, we can choose friends in our lives and choose to create a significant relationship that reflects who we are and what we have always wanted. We can create a new family now that fulfills our dreams and desires. This does not mean rejecting our original family, but learning from it, still giving to it, but at the same time going forward to create our lives as we wish them to be.

Today's Diet
MAKE PEACE WITH YOUR FAMILY

When we recognize that we are carrying so many of the patterns of our past and what a burden they are, it is easy to start letting go. Unless and until we come to peace with our family, it is inevitable that we will be caught in the past. We will experience the rejection we received in our family over and over again. We will crave the love and approval we craved then, and demand it inappropriately in our present-day lives. Even when we may receive it, it will not fill the deep loss we may feel from not having received it in childhood. The only way to resolve that loss is to face where these needs are coming from. One of the greatest gifts you can give both yourself and family members is to begin the process of making peace.

STEP 1: *Acknowledgment.*

1. Describe each member of the family, what you wanted from them, and how you wanted them to be.
2. Acknowledge each member of the family for who they were.
3. Allow them to be exactly who they were. Realize that who they were was not a reflection of you.
4. Describe how you were in the family.

5. Allow yourself also to be exactly as you were, no matter what others felt about you.

6. Describe what each family member gave you, and the ways in which they supported your life.

7. Describe what you gave them.

STEP 2: *Giving Thanks.*

1. Write a formal thank-you letter to each member of the family for something important you received from him or her.

2. Are there any gifts you may want to give these family members? Give one today.

STEP 3: *Apologize.*

Once wrongs are righted, we have gone a long way toward letting go of anger and feeling good about ourselves. Contrary to popular opinion, we do not need to receive the apologies of others as much as we need to apologize to feel free and happy and allow ourselves to go forward in life.

1. Rather than dwell upon how they hurt or disappointed you, look and see if there may be some way you need to apologize to someone for something. If there is, do it. Write a note of apology. Ask for forgiveness. Even if the offense took place a long time ago, this will be very healing for you. It will also mean a great deal to them.

2. Find out how you can make it up now. (You can ask, or think of a way to make recompense.) Now, do it. If you cannot make recompense to a member of your own family, perhaps you can do this with someone else.

STEP 4: *Create a New Family.*

Describe your highest values for how a family can be. What is it you want to experience in a family? Choose friends and create relationships that reflect this now.

Anger in the Workplace

He who requires much from himself and little from others
will keep himself from being the object of resentment.

— CONFUCIUS

ANGER OFTEN ERUPTS in the workplace. Sometimes its expression is subtle and other times not. In the most extreme form, we see enraged employees acting out and killing those they feel have wronged them. Fortunately, anger usually functions in a much more subtle way. It appears in the form of competition, exclusion, domination, power plays, and many other forms of behavior that are considered acceptable in a business context. Even though it may be socially acceptable for an employer to treat an employee harshly, nevertheless this is still abuse, a manifestation of anger, and it inevitably has negative effects both upon the one being angry and the one being abused.

Being at the receiving end of anger is dispiriting. It removes enthusiasm, creativity, and the desire to give one's best. Inevitably, sooner or later the employee will find a way to retaliate—often in the quality or quantity of work done. The one in charge who feels entitled to dominate or abuse others also suffers toxic effects. That individual must live with their own anger. Sooner or later it affects their body, mind, and general well-being. And, anger given forth, inevitably returns to oneself.

Cara was a gifted employee—enthusiastic, dedicated, and willing to work long past the hours required of her. Her immediate superior took notice of this and became uneasy. She felt intimidated by Cara's success and the attention she was generating in the company. She even felt that Cara might well be after her job. The insecure boss then undertook a systematic program of intimidating Cara, finding every fault or mistake Cara made, and then scolding her for it, often publicly. Cara couldn't believe what was happening. No matter how hard she tried or how much she gave, her boss always found something missing and wrong. She refused to allow Cara to get ahead.

Before long Cara's work began to slide. She began coming in later, taking longer lunches, and finding reasons to leave earlier. Her sick days increased as well. This naturally generated more criticism from her boss. Cara grew increasingly uneasy and unable to concentrate. The boss was getting the results she was after, diminishing Cara's self-esteem, balance, and ability to do well. Before long, Cara was fired and the boss felt that her main competitor had been eliminated.

Socially Approved Anger

Due to the hierarchical nature of most workplaces, supervisors and bosses have certain rights with regard to the employee. They have the right to supervise their work and ensure a certain level of productivity and performance. This right to supervise can be used to justify scoldings, badgering, harassment, and other forms of anger, expressed at an individual who is under their control and is dependent on getting their approval in order to remain employed. Employees are naturally dependent upon the good opinion of their superiors, and must please them to get ahead. Their very livelihood may be at stake. This situation lends itself to a delicate balance, where domination, control, manipulation, and other forms of anger can easily be expressed. The nature of this unequal relationship is one that seems to give certain individuals permission to express anger that could not be expressed elsewhere.

Needless to say, it is crucial to be aware of the inherent dangers of this relationship and work to defuse them.

Misplaced Anger

Beyond the socially approved anger that can be expressed in the workplace, there is a much deeper issue here. Individuals who work together spend more time with one another than they do with members of their families or friends. In this context it is inevitable that transferences will take place. A transference is a projection of feelings onto an individual that has nothing to do with them.

For example, being with any group of people continually will begin to call forth family dynamics. Unconsciously, the feelings and behavior one learned in one's family constellation will begin to emerge. Different people in the workplace will become stand-ins for significant individuals in one's past. A person will be reminded, consciously or unconsciously, of her father, mother, or siblings. The same psychological dynamics that went on in the original family will now begin to be acted out. Often this all takes place outside of awareness.

One can recognize this happening when an individual begins to react inappropriately to someone they are working with. Some signs of this include fear of an authority, an excessive need to please, and anger, frustration, or critical behavior toward someone. Due to the great amount of time spent together it is very probable that anger that was not acknowledged or expressed in the past will become activated in one way or another in the workplace situation.

It is a great art to delineate anger that is appropriate to a present-day circumstance and anger that is a projection from the past. If the anger is from the past, no matter what the individual in the current situation does to correct it, the anger remains. This misplaced or projected anger is the source of a great deal of the anxiety, stress, and acting out that goes on in the workplace.

The Craving for Success

Another source of anger in the workplace arises from the intense competition that is often generated. Some individuals want to succeed so badly that they feel most others to be a threat that needs to be eliminated one way or another. Their orientation toward others is filled with anger, scheming, and the willingness to cut anyone's throat along the way. Competition that gets out of hand is a great source of anger, both in the person who is competing and in their opponent.

Many companies feel that competition leads to greater performance and productivity. They do not care about the quality of their employees' lives, only about the bottom line. Other organizations realize that the richest results come about through creating teamwork and a win-win attitude. It is crucial to be aware of the company culture one operates in. The ones that are fueled by anger and excessive competition ultimately exact a heavy price from those who work there.

Today's Diet
MAKE A COMPETITOR INTO AN ALLY

It is enormously helpful to stop a moment and take stock of the extent to which anger and competition are the fuels that keep your workday going. If you are driven by the need to succeed, it is crucial to understand what success means to you. Is it defined by outdoing others or knocking them out of the playing field? Does this kind of modus operandi result in a life that you enjoy living? What toll is it taking?

STEP 1: *Find a Competitor.*

Whom do you compete with at work? Choose the one that gives you the most trouble. Write down what it is that you want to win. Write your feelings about the person and the ways in which the two of you compete. Who wins most often? When you win, how do you feel?

STEP 2: *Let Others Win.*

Let your competitor win today. (If they are a client you negotiate with—give them what they're wanting.) Fill this particular day with goodwill toward your opponent. Find ways to help them. Let them know at least one thing you care for and respect about them.

See how you feel after this day. Who is the real winner?

STEP 3: *Success or Failure.*

Write down what success means to you. How about failure? What do you require to feel that you have succeeded? Do you ever really succeed? How about failure? How often do you consider that you have failed? Are these standards helpful? Are they realistic? Take a moment and see if you could take a recent failure and view it as a success.

STEP 4: *Create a Win-Win Environment.*

See what it takes to create a situation at work where everybody wins. How would that be possible? Visualize a day like that and describe it. See what the quality of life would be in such a situation. How much is that worth to you?

Anger with Governments and Organizations

In the path a man wishes to follow he is led.

— Chesbon Ha Nefesh

As we have seen, when anger is not acknowledged, owned, or experienced it becomes repressed. Repressed anger is a time bomb waiting to detonate. The nature of repressed anger is that it must be released. The way this most frequently happens is that it is projected outside the individual onto the surrounding world.

The Projection of Anger

Individuals filled with the pressure of repressed anger live in a world that becomes filled with danger, cruelty, and objects of hate. This repressed anger finds many places, causes, and organizations that it deems to be fully worthy of its hatred. Many justifications are developed for spewing this anger and working toward the downfall of various governments, organizations, and individuals.

Demonstrations, political causes, vicious reporting, and the like can often be traced to personal anger and vendettas that are waiting to erupt.

This is not to say that there are not just and worthy causes of demonstrations, political causes, and the like. It is crucial to make a distinction between appropriate responses to public and civic issues and responses that are fueled by the repressed rage of individuals waiting to explode.

Ray and his siblings were badly abused by his father for many years. As the oldest child, he felt particularly responsible for the suffering of his family. The father dominated each person with threats, beatings, rages, and the constant declaration that he was the final authority and in charge of what went on. Ray's mother was passive and dependent and unable to stand up to his father or serve as protection for herself or her children.

Throughout his life Ray vacillated between feeling terrified and powerless, and dreaming up schemes of revenge in which he saw his father conquered. He saw himself taking over the reins of the family and finally caring for his siblings. While Ray lived at home, these fantasies remained simply dreams. His father was too overpowering a figure for Ray to confront. However, as soon as he left home, Ray's smoldering sense of injustice became directed against the government. He became involved in political causes and wrote diatribes against various figures who he felt were abusing the trust of their constituents.

Ray combed the news for stories of individuals such as these in governments all over the world. He particularly enjoyed becoming involved in demonstrations, especially when there was the possibility of violence.

Clearly, Ray's feelings toward his father were being projected upon those in authority in the government. As he had the support of his political group, this was a place where Ray felt empowered to take action, to justify his behavior, and to finally get release from his feelings of helplessness and rage.

Impersonal Anger

Although Ray's case may be a bit extreme, it is a wonderful example of the dynamics of projected anger, particularly toward governments and organizations of various kinds. The large and impersonal nature of governments and organizations allows an individual such as Ray to feel comfortable and justified in blaming those involved in them. They do not know these individuals they are attacking personally, but only through their public personas. This is a wonderful opportunity to project anger and whatever else they imagine. Rarely do they have to come face to face with these individuals, so anonymity is also provided. Although there may certainly be seeds of truth in what Ray perceives, these seeds are blown up out of proportion and are triggered by memories of his past ill treatment.

All kinds of public figures can easily become the recipients of the projections of others and often do. Not only individuals but governments and organizations that stand for something that is in opposition to what an individual believes in, or support actions that an individual feels reprehensible, can easily become the targets for repressed rage.

Once again, this is not to say that there are not justifiable causes for anger and action to be taken, but when reactions become excessive, or when anger erupts easily, without knowing much about the background, facts, or full picture of the government, policy, or organization, it is wise to realize that projection is operating.

In keeping with this, a great deal of the fear that is felt when a new government takes power is often related to childhood fears, projected now upon the government. Our families were given the charge of keeping us safe, protected, and cared for. If this trust was betrayed and we felt unsafe, or in an unjust environment, these old feelings are easily evoked and directed toward the organizations or governments we are involved with now who have similar functions in our lives.

Anger with Authorities

When we see excess anger with governments and organizations, usually a fundamental part of the pattern arises from trouble with authorities. The experience of having been controlled, dominated, demeaned, or obstructed by an authority figure at home, in school, or in church creates a great impact. Wounds are often left that make it difficult to function later on, in adulthood. A deep mistrust of authorities arises, often accompanied by rage at having been betrayed or deeply disappointed.

Positive authority is crucial for children as they grow. They need role models and heroes to look up to, love, respect, and fashion their lives after. Children initially and naturally grant this adulation and respect to the adults (authorities) in their lives. It is a precious trust. When this trust is misused, when children are harmed, betrayed, and disappointed, not only do they develop anger with authorities in general, but also they often have difficulty in becoming an authority in their own lives. This makes it difficult or impossible to grow into full adulthood and take on the responsibilities that go along with it. Instead, entire lives are spent in rebellion. Rather than feel that an authority figure will be a source of guidance, support, or inspiration, they are viewed as opponents who will take away autonomy, creativity, and the individual's right to be who they are.

Becoming the Authority in One's Own Life

Authority worship and hatred for authority are two sides of the same coin. Both arise from attachment to external authorities and the inability to become the authority in one's own life. Both of these orientations are disempowering and keep the individual in a childlike state, with the need for someone to look after them.

In the process of growing into full maturity, it is crucial to be able to feel on an equal par with authorities, to take back the power one has projected onto them and ultimately be able to assume responsibility in one's own life. When one is able to do this, much anger towards others dissolves and one is then free to use the energy to develop one's life and values in a constructive, healthy way.

Today's Diet
BECOME YOUR OWN AUTHORITY

When we validate ourselves and take responsibility for our actions and choices, new possibilities and good feelings are released into our lives. This is a step many people have not yet taken, no matter how many years they have lived. Many still remain unconsciously entangled with organizations and authorities that do not empower them and keep unconscious anger brewing.

STEP 1: *Who Is the Authority in Your Life?*

Take a moment and write a list of the "authorities" in your life. What is it you give power to? What is it you respect? Now, the crucial question: Are these authorities constructive for you? Are they a source of encouragement, health, and inspiration, or are they a source of negative feelings about yourself, resulting in self-punishment?

(In doing this exercise, you can include individuals, beliefs, organizations, governments, etc.)

Step 2: *Eliminate Negative Authorities.*

This step may seem quite difficult. In fact, it isn't. All that is needed is to carefully look at the effects a particular authority has upon you. Write it all down. Pick one authority that is not positive and spend time writing down all the ways it has hampered your well-being.

Many so-called authorities are actually negative forces, masquerading as though they had special power, wisdom, or validity. One of the main tasks of maturity is uncovering these negative authorities and replacing them with ones that are positive and sustaining.

As we sort through the effects of the different authorities, it becomes easy to let go of that which is destructive and to see it for what it is. As we continue this process, our anger with governments and organizations will diminish greatly and assume appropriate forms. We will not be projecting the negative authorities from our own lives onto them.

By their fruits will ye know them.

— THE NEW TESTAMENT

STEP 3: *Establish Positive Influences*

Now, after you look at your list of negative authorities in your life, replace one a day with a positive influence. A positive influence would be something, some person, belief, activity, you look up to and respect. Something that is life-giving for you.

In doing this you are now taking back power from the negative authorities and assuming responsibility for what you do and do not value, for that which is life-giving and meaningful to you. You no longer feel like the *victim* of the world you live in. You are empowered now to *make choices* about that which you do and do not accept. This is a vital function of maturity, one that children and those who live their lives at the effect of anger cannot assume.

Prejudice— Anger at Different Sexual Orientations, Races, and Religions

Let your fellow's honor be as dear to you
as your own, and do not anger easily.

— JOHANAN BEN ZAKKAI, first-century Palestinian Jewish sage

UNFORTUNATELY, much of our education and upbringing leads to the development of prejudice. In a search for value and identity we identify ourselves as part of one group, separate and distinct from another. Not only do we see ourselves as separate and distinct, but we attribute all the good qualities and all the fine virtues in life to the group we belong to. Very often we attribute all the negatives—aspects we reject such as our fears and hatreds—to members of other groups. These other groups are to be demeaned and kept in their place, as they are somehow dangerous. These groups are consigned to the back of the bus, literally and figuratively. Not only are they rejected and kept away from our lives, but they become fit figures for abuse and violence of all kinds. This is the origin of hate crimes. This is the origin of war.

Reginald was a solid upstanding citizen. He was well known within his community where he was raised and where he returned after college. Strongly identified with his race, religion, and family, he had little tolerance for anything that fell outside of the parameters of his comfortable world. Not only that, Reginald secretly found members of other cultures and races disagreeable, as they did not follow his mores and did not hold similar values. He often said under his breath that these people were simply "barbarians," not sufficiently evolved to be taken true notice of.

When a family of a different race and religion purchased a home on Reginald's block, he became increasingly anxious, feeling invaded and unsafe. He refused to allow them to join various organizations in the community. Reginald locked his doors tight at night and would not greet these neighbors. Finally, his life became so uncomfortable that he sold his home and moved his family.

Prejudice and Identity

Reginald's reaction was not only based upon social conditioning and his false sense of superiority, it was based upon his fragile identity. He did not really know who he was. He had no idea what his real place in life was and he did not feel secure within his own existence. Reginald had constructed a man-made identity—a wall around him composed of his identification with his group. In order to live in a world of his liking, he created a prison without bars. He could not escape it and no one could reach him inside.

Just as he did not know himself, Reginald was unable to see others for who they were. He was involved with projection in the extreme, only seeing individuals as symbols. This way of perceiving others took their humanity from them and took Reginald's humanity from him as well. Reginald's identity was not organic and flexible but simply a symbol of who he believed he should be.

Projecting the Shadow

Another fundamental aspect of prejudice, whether it be against those of a different religion, race, or sexual orientation, is what we call "projecting the shadow."

According to the noted psychologist Robert Bly, the shadow part of an individual is that which they cannot accept about themselves. For example, if an individual is filled with anger that he represses, he projects it on those individuals who are "ostensibly" different—those of a different religion, race, or sexual orientation. People who project their shadow in this way perceive members of a different group as angry and dangerous. What is really dangerous is their own repressed anger, but it has been rejected, and projected outside themselves. By rejecting the group that holds their projection, they are rejecting the anger that lives within them.

This process is true not only of anger but also of greed, sexuality, and whatever feels dark and unacceptable in life. Those who are homophobic are often projecting their fear, rejection, and hatred of their own homosexual impulses upon those who are gay. By ridiculing and punishing gay individuals they are attempting to expunge their own homosexual impulses and feelings.

Needless to say, this projection process goes on very strongly when it comes to individuals of different religions. Many scriptures speak of the various "enemies of God." It is only too easy to view those who do not share beliefs and values as belonging to that group. As a result, much killing, torture, and misery has happened in the name of God. One simply labels a member of a different religion as an enemy of God and this justifies abuse and madness of all kinds.

If we stop and look carefully at all scripture, it is easy to see our common values and also to realize that the true enemy of God is the confusion and pain we live in.

Eating the Shadow

Once again, rather than projecting our shadow upon others, it is necessary to turn within and realize that all the darkness we see outside ourselves also lives within. By becoming aware of our own dark side, or negativity, by taking responsibility and releasing it, not only we but all people are able to be who they are, and to be valued as well. Then it is possible for all to live in peace and harmony. The differences between individuals or groups then are not a source of alarm, but of beauty. We see the manifestation of our common humanity in many different forms. At that time the true directive of all scriptures is fulfilled.

Love thy neighbor as thyself.

—THE OLD TESTAMENT

Today's Diet
GET TO KNOW SOMEONE
YOU ARE PREJUDICED AGAINST

Rather than live with the projections we have placed upon other people, today we will begin the wonderful work of taking the masks and costumes off. Some will be amazed to discover who and what they are prejudiced against. Many live with secret prejudices that create fear and anger and that never see the light of day. This anger, naturally, becomes expressed in other ways and impedes harmony in one's life.

STEP 1: *Uncovering Our Prejudices.*

Make a list of the groups you feel uneasy about. If you don't know who they are, look around and see individuals you do not have as friends, or those you would go out of your way not to be in a relationship with. Be honest with yourself. No one will see what you are writing.

STEP 2: *Taking Off the Mask.*

Look within and ask yourself honestly what it is about individuals from those groups that truly bothers you. Write a description of that person as you imagine them to be.

Now write a description of yourself in that area. Can you find similarities between you and that person? Is it possible that what they are expressing is something you're hiding from? Why are those qualities so objectionable? Spend time with this question. It can open many doors.

STEP 3: *Get to Know Someone You Are Prejudiced Against.*

This is an amazingly simple and wonderful exercise. I have seen it change many lives. All that is required is to actually spend a little time with someone you have been prejudiced against. Go to a meeting where these individuals are present. Read their newspapers. Shop in some stores they shop in. Be present in their world.

Find a specific individual and spend a little time talking with them about their life and what is important to them.

The task here is to find the common humanity between you and them and to see your projections for what they are.

Whether or not you choose to continue any relationship, this will give you much freedom. You will realize the enormous power the mind has to obstruct, delude, and turn something into what it is not. That is the road to freedom from the real enemy of life.

CHAPTER 30 • *Day 25*

Review and Repair

Today's Diet
REVIEW OF THE PAST FOUR DAYS

STEP 1: *The Most Meaningful Ideas*

Write down the most meaningful ideas of the past four days to you. What about them touched you?

STEP 2: *The Most Meaningful Exercises*

Which exercises were most meaningful to you? Why? Would you like to make some adjustments to them? It's fine. Do it. It's wonderful to take what suits you and fine-tune it. We are all different. A little adjustment here or there makes it your own.

STEP 3: *The Most Difficult Exercises*

Which exercises were most difficult? Were there some you could not or would not do? That's fine as well. It's to be expected. It's also extremely valuable to notice which ones they were. Take a little while to reflect upon this. What was it about these exercises that was so difficult or unpleasant to

you? Can you see how doing them might make a difference in your life? Would you be willing to try even one of them? Would you be willing to do one today?

STEP 4: *The Most Meaningful Interaction*
As we undertake these exercises, new and meaningful interactions take place. It is inevitable. Write down what happened to you. Describe your meaningful interactions. What else happened between you and others? It's good to keep a record. As we go through this program it will become fascinating to look back and follow the trail we have gone along.

STEP 5: *Changes That Are Needed*
Write what changes you notice are needed in your life as you have gone through these past few days. Don't be afraid to write down anything that you think of. You will not have to do them all at once. Just make a note of them. Simply realizing that changes are needed is a huge step. Most of us don't take time to pay attention to this. Acknowledge yourself for being willing to be aware of changes that may need to take place.

STEP 6: *Actions That Are Needed*
As we do these exercises we can become aware of people we haven't called or contacted, gifts we haven't given, projects we've left unfinished, dreams we've left unfulfilled. It's

helpful to write these down. Just make a list. Don't become overwhelmed by it. Just write it down.

STEP 7: *Changes That Have Taken Place*

As we go through these days we will also become aware of natural, spontaneous changes that have taken place in the way we see things and relate to others. Write these down. They're fascinating. Many happen all by themselves.

STEP 8: *Actions That Have Taken Place*

Just as changes have naturally taken place, we most likely have taken many new actions. Keep a record of these. It is very easy for things we do to slip away. If we do not take time to notice and record our actions, they escape our view. The more we notice and become aware of what is going on, the more power it has in our lives and the lives of others. We also receive encouragement and inspiration by taking time to realize and absorb what is happening.

STEP 9: *New Possibilities*

Here is our chance to write down any new steps we may wish to take. Anything can be included, in any area of our lives. As we go through this program, new desires, goals, hopes, and possibilities will be arising. Don't let them slip away. What are the new possibilities that are appearing on your horizon? Write them down. Give them life.

STEP 10: *New Promises*

Do you want to make a promise to yourself today? This is a strong resolution that is important to you. Promises have power. Keeping a promise is even more empowering than making one. Start off by making a promise you can keep. See how it feels to keep it.

STEP 11: *Wins*

Here is the place where you list your gains in well-being. The mind naturally wants to negate change, progress, and new steps. By taking time to review and repair what is going on we turn that process around. We acknowledge what we are doing and what its consequences are in our lives. As you do this, you will be amazed at how many ways you win. What you focus upon increases, and the more you focus upon your wins, not your losses, the more they will appear in your life.

Happy sailing.

Anger with the Self: Suicide

*The real battle is inner, and is nothing
but a battle between the real and ideal man.*

— Buddhist saying

SUICIDE IS ONE OF THE MOST PAINFUL and far-reaching manifestations of anger, and one that has devastating effects not only upon its victim but upon friends and family as well. Sadly, we see a rising tide of teenage suicide these days. This phenomenon not only shakes the foundation of the family, but leaves survivors profoundly shaken, wondering how the suicide could have been prevented, what causes led up to it, and in what ways they were to blame. Guilt after the suicide of a close one can last for years, ruining relationships and joy in life.

Anna and her husband could not function after the suicide of their teenage son. Both of them worked full-time and over the years spent only limited time at home. They blamed themselves for everything and spent hours going over what happened and what they could have done. Ultimately, the marriage ended, as do the marriages of many where there is the suicide of a child. The couple could no longer bear facing each other; they were only reminded of what had happened.

When Anna came for therapy her life was in tatters. It took a while for her to begin to realize that she had a right to live and go forward with her life, even though her son had not been able to. She also had to find a way to give back to other children and families who were facing the threat of that happening to them.

Although it is difficult to talk about suicide, it is necessary to open it up and try to understand some of the contributory factors, and how we can catch them before they grow out of hand. Suicide is the peak of anger that has been allowed to fester for too long.

Why Suicide?

The act of suicide goes against our natural biological impulse to survive, to take care of others and ourselves. On the surface it would seem that suicide would be undertaken only rarely, in the most extreme circumstances. It is hard for many to understand how this final and drastic measure has become so prevalent these days.

To begin to understand suicide, it is necessary to understand that there are many kinds of pain individuals suffer: physical pain, emotional pain, social pain, and spiritual pain. When their pain becomes unmanageable, there is the common illusion that suicide will end it all. There is also the common feeling that by killing oneself one will show others how they have let one down, that others will be sorry. Others will finally suffer the way the victim has been suffering all along. When the expression of anger is unacceptable, when individuals have perfectionist standards to meet, when there is no one present to really listen and accept all aspects of the individual's life, hopelessness and suicide become a possibility.

Suicide and Revenge

It is impossible to speak truthfully about suicide without making mention of the rage that underlies this behavior. Suicide and homicide are two sides of the same coin. The individual is contemplating murder. Because they cannot murder others, because they cannot express their rage in any acceptable way, the anger becomes turned toward themselves. For many, the act of killing themselves is a way of hurting others, getting back at them. It is also a cry for attention and to be taken seriously. Many victims of suicide begin to feel helpless and unable to get the response from the world they desire. They see no other way to have an effect or to get what they want. Through suicide they feel they will get the attention, peace, or revenge they have so long desired.

Suicide and Manipulation

Suicide can be used as an extreme means of control. Some suicidal individuals desperately want to get their way. They want to have an effect upon others and use the "threat" of suicide as a way to keep others in line. Some threaten to kill themselves if people they are close to act in a way that displeases them. This is the ultimate manipulation. It is suicide used as blackmail.

For others suicide is a way to manipulate life itself. As there is nothing else the individual feels they can control, at least they have control over their own life and death. Their suicides can be a statement that they are not simply a twig blowing in the wind but can take a measure to gain control over what is happening to them.

Suicide and Loneliness

Many suicidal individuals are the victims of deep feelings of loneliness, estrangement, and meaninglessness. They have no sense of being part of a meaningful community or of the fabric of life. They cannot see how they can participate or make a difference. Their lives seem worthless and empty to them.

The profound loneliness these individuals suffer has also been described by the existentialist psychologist Rollo May as "shut-up-ness." This is the condition of being shut up within oneself, disconnected and isolated, unable to make oneself known. Often if there is the sense that just one other individual really sees and hears them, just one other individual who they could help or impact upon, suicidal desires fade into the background.

Suicide and Attention

Some have no other way than suicide to get the attention they need. Rather than grasping the actual consequences of their act, they fantasize about what will happen when they are dead: the people who will find them, how they will be sobbing, how they'll finally realize how important the person was. They fantasize about their funerals and how their significant others will finally be wondering about what they could have done differently. All of the fantasies of these individuals are based around getting the attention, love, or understanding that they haven't been able to get in life. The reality of what they are doing, or what will really happen, eludes them entirely.

Suicide's Warning Signals

So often there are warning signals that are not picked up or understood for what they are. It is very helpful to realize that these warning signals are pleas for help. They should not be taken lightly. Even one person can make a difference if they intervene in the right time and the right manner.

Withdrawal

If you notice that an individual is withdrawing, spending significantly more time alone, and becoming more uncommunicative, be aware. This often is the result of feelings of helplessness and lack of ability to be heard. It is also a sign of an individual's retreating from life and entering more deeply into their own dreams.

Suicidal Ideation

If an individual speaks about suicide, thinks about it, dwells upon it, and threatens it, take this seriously. You may think they are saying it in jest, but if this subject is coming up, it means that it is brewing within. This individual needs special attention, time, and care.

Difficulty with Sleeping, Eating

When an individual begins to have difficulty with basic life functions, not only is it a sign of depression and anxiety, but often also includes suicidal feelings. There is deep agitation and unrest here, which must be handled carefully.

Losses or Significant Failures

Some individuals react very badly to losses, repeated losses, or significant failures and disappointments. They take such events to mean that they are worthless and do not deserve to live. They also may not feel able to function without a person they have lost, or if there has been a death of someone to whom they are very close, such as a beloved spouse, they may wish to join the person in death.

Today's Diet

PAY ATTENTION TO THOSE IN YOUR WORLD

Today's diet calls for increasing awareness of the suffering of others in your world, and becoming alerted to any dire situations that could be brewing, particularly related to suicide.

STEP 1: *Open Up Your Eyes and Ears.*

Take time to really look at and listen to people in your world. Has someone you know recently had a significant loss? Is there illness in someone's family? Do you notice that an individual may be withdrawing and out of touch?

Make contact with that person. Let them know you are there for them. Take time to talk with them; take them out to dinner or lunch or a movie. Keep in touch. Often just knowing someone is there and really concerned makes a huge difference. It can be a bridge between handling the situation and feeling overwhelmed.

STEP 2: *Don't Run Away.*

Usually when someone expresses great distress or suicidal ideation our impulse is to run away, or to try to cheer him or her up. This only makes the individual feel worse, thinking they have not really been heard or taken seriously.

If someone is expressing this kind of behavior, really listen to him or her. Let them know you've heard how they're hurting. Let them know help is available. Then, make every effort to notify their family, or to get that person proper help. It may be too difficult for them to do research to find a good therapist or psychiatrist. Do it for them. Present them with some alternatives. Give them the resources they need and offer to go with them if need be. Pay attention to the warning signals listed above. This kind of care and attention can save someone's life.

STEP 3: *Helping the Family.*
If a suicide has taken place, realize that the family members are now hurting as much as the victim was. This is a time for offering your presence and any support they can accept. Just being there and listening does a great deal. Do not try to take their guilt away. Do not give all kinds of reasons to explain what happened.

At the early stages, the family simply needs someone to be at their side and listen to them without judgment and without offering explanations of all kinds. Usually the best way families of suicide victims get help is in being with other families who have gone through this as well and can relate to the suffering they are going through.

Anger at God and the Universe

*One word frees us from all the weight
and pain of life; that word is love.*

— SOPHOCLES

ALTHOUGH THIS IS A DIFFICULT TOPIC to discuss, anger at God or the Universe is an underpinning of some individuals' lives. Beneath all of their actions is a running battle with or resentment toward God and the universe. These individuals feel as though they are toys or playthings in the hands of God. God has all the power and they have little control or say over what happens. Beyond that, some feel as though they must obey all of God's directives or receive great punishment. No matter how much they do or how good they are, it is never enough. They still cannot win.

Berta was a devout Christian who went to church regularly, read her Bible, gave to charity, and participated in organizations dedicated to helping the poor. She lived a solemn and modest life and did what she felt was required of her. In the middle of her life, at around age forty, her husband suddenly left for someone else, one of her children became addicted to drugs, and the minister upon whom she had depended died in a car accident.

Not only was Berta's faith sorely shaken, but great anger and resentment arose. Although her friends told her she was being tested, this idea did not help. Berta dwelled upon all the good she had done and how she did not deserve this. She questioned over and over how God could have let this happen. Beyond that, Berta also began dwelling upon all the good times she felt she had missed and the opportunities that had slipped by her because she was following God's will.

Berta's life became filled with anger toward God for what He had done. She also directed anger at herself for not seeing what was coming. In Berta's case she felt as though she had been duped. She never questioned the ways in which she thought about God or what the larger meaning of these events was in her life. Berta saw herself totally as an unsuspecting victim. She finally concluded that she was being punished, but she did not know exactly for what.

Perceptions of God and the Universe

Our fundamental ideas about God and the universe determine the way we receive, understand, and respond to the many events that occur in our lives. If an individual feels deeply out of control and does not see the relationship between his or her own actions, thoughts, and deeds and what happens to them, they can easily resort to blaming God for everything.

One image of God is of a stern and punishing force that constantly watches and judges our behavior and thoughts and metes out just responses. Our behavior is then dictated by fear, as is our relationship to God. It can be difficult to love and feel close to a God that one fears. It can even be difficult to respond out of love to others or to behave naturally and spontaneously if we are always on the alert for what we may have done wrong.

This perception of God is based upon an implicit belief in a dualistic universe, one where we are separate from God, where our lives and thoughts are under His control, where we are constantly being tested, and where we are always engaged in the struggle of good against evil. When this is our perception of God, it is understandable to feel anger and the sense of living under a threat and feeling of doom.

Other perceptions of God and other relationships to God have different effects on the individual and the way in which he or she lives. When we truly perceive God and the universe as benevolent and merciful, as a source of plenty and of forgiveness, we respond to life with much less anger and distress. God then becomes an unconditionally loving parent to whom we can always return. The mistakes we make are not necessarily sins or crimes, but ways in which we learn. They can be acknowledged, accounted for, and repaired. We do not see ourselves as fundamentally evil. We have a right to breathe, to love, and to be fully here.

Relationship to God, Oneself, and Others

There are three distinct relationships we have during our lives: to God and the universe, to oneself, and to others. Most of the time these three relationships are confused and this confusion generates a sense of being unfulfilled, of frustration and anger. When we become clear about each of these relationships, what to expect from each one, what to turn to each relationship for, much anger and distress dissolves.

We then no longer turn to others for that which we need from God. We no longer turn to God for that which we need from ourselves. We no longer turn to ourselves for that which we need from others. When we go to the right place to have our needs met, it is easy to find fulfillment.

In Berta's case, she blamed God for difficulty in her relationships with others, where she herself had to intervene to become aware of what was taking place, communicate, and be able to give and receive. There were choices she had to make about what was and was not right for her life. These are actions and choices that a person cannot simply delegate to God.

We do not know the details of Berta's unhappy marriage, but it is possible she turned to her husband for some strength that she needed to receive both from God and from herself. Spending time alone with oneself is crucial. We need to know who we are, to listen to what our heart says and find time to fulfill its desires and directives. We also need time to commune with the Godhead and receive the enlightenment, insight, love, and fulfillment that are fundamental to who we are. One relationship cannot substitute for another. If we try to make this happen, it becomes easy to blame God or the universe for all our woes.

Coming to Terms

Each individual has the personal responsibility to come to terms with what they believe their purpose in this life is—and to live it. Each one has to discover values and life directions that express the essence of who they are. To simply follow along blindly is to escape from this crucial life task.

Just as there are no two sets of fingerprints that are alike, so there are no two individuals who are exactly alike in their gifts, trials, strengths, and duties. Not coming to terms—not truly knowing oneself and not living a life based upon one's true foundation—leads to anger, bitterness, and cruelty.

Anger with God and the universe is often anger with oneself that is projected upon God, or upon some idea of what God is or isn't. Anger with God is often the result of not coming to terms with who we are and what is wanted of us. It is easy to blame a faraway God, and not stop and look right inside at how we are living, thinking, and responding each day of our lives.

Today's Diet
MAKE FRIENDS WITH GOD AND THE UNIVERSE

Once we develop a personal relationship to God and the universe, our fruitless anger at life itself dissipates greatly.

STEP 1: *Spend Time Alone with God and the Universe.*

We spend so much time running after many things and people and seldom take time alone to be with God and the universe. Take some time today. Stop running, seclude yourself for a little while, and spend time with God and the universe. Talk aloud, meditate upon Him, ask for guidance, study meaningful scripture or literature, whatever it is that is meaningful to you. Let go of the endless concerns with everyday life and commune with the source and essence of your life.

STEP 2: *Forgive God and the Universe for Whatever Pain You Have Suffered.*

Whether or not you consciously feel that God and the universe are the cause of your suffering, this is a wonderful exercise. Take time to forgive God, to let go of anger and blame, to extend an olive branch. See what is needed in order for you to be able to do this.

STEP 3: *Spend Time Alone with Yourself.*

Spend time alone with yourself. Look and listen within. Sense what you are sensing; follow your breathing. Find out what is going on inside. Make friends with who you are. Accept what you are feeling, thinking, and seeing. Stop judging yourself and let yourself be known. There is nothing as good for releasing anger as becoming intimate and accepting of yourself. The more you do this, the less anger you will feel at the entire world.

STEP 4: *Make an Offering.*

Think about what it is that you can and want to offer to God and the universe. Usually we dwell upon what we want to receive. Most of our actions involve bargaining. This is an opportunity to see what you want to offer. Offer it unconditionally.

Anger at Destiny

*There is a natural magnetism
which selects for each what belongs to it.*

— EMERSON

SOME INDIVIDUALS FOCUS their outrage with life on destiny. They feel that fate has dealt them a bad blow and there is nothing they can do about it. No matter what they try, how they want to change, how many efforts they make, they are doomed to failure. Their lives are ultimately in the hands of blind destiny.

The Many Faces of Destiny

When asked exactly what *destiny* is, some describe their genetics. They feel they have inherited physical qualities that determine their capacities and what happens to them. As these qualities are set before their birth, there is little they can do.

Others consider destiny to have the quality of luck. What happens to them is based on the luck of the draw.

The world for these individuals is basically random. Rabbits' feet and other kinds of amulets can bring forth better luck. But basically these individuals have little control over the consequences of their actions. Those who think this way either become passive, hopeless, and resigned to misery or excessively willful and controlling, to counteract the helplessness they feel.

For those who feel that life has order and actions produce consequences, some subscribe to the idea of karma. Karma is based upon cause and effect. As you sow, so shall you reap. One's thoughts, speech, and actions become the seeds of karma sown. Even seeds sown in a previous life will come to bloom when the right conditions present themselves. Karma does not always manifest immediately; the chain of cause and effect and also of mitigating conditions can be quite complex. Individuals who believe in karma are more careful about their thoughts, words, and actions, feeling that one day they will reap the consequences of them.

Others believe that their destiny or fate is in the hands of God. There is a divine intelligence that has worked out the course of their lives. They must not only be accountable to the divine but also be diligent about leading a life that makes them worthy of divine favor, or grace. Although some feel that divine grace cannot be earned, nevertheless a strong awareness of God, a fear of repercussions, or a sense of the holiness of life itself guides these individuals' footsteps.

When Destiny Is Against Us

Anna was married three times. Each one of them ended badly. In the beginning things went well and both partners were happy. At about the three-year mark in all the relationships, the men became restless and bored with Anna and found someone else. Anna could not believe the way this pattern repeated itself relentlessly.

"It is my horrible destiny," she declared. "I am doomed to be a woman scorned."

The more Anna believed this, the more paralyzed she became. She no longer tried to meet new men. She stopped wondering about her part in the events that took place. When it was suggested that perhaps her beliefs, behaviors, or unconscious patterns contributed to the outcome, she refused to listen. Anna also had no interest in exploring what she had learned from her experiences. Everything was blamed upon destiny. There was no other way for her to cope with what went on.

Although Anna may have received temporary solace from denying her role in the events, her way of responding turned her into a victim and disempowered her when it came to living the rest of her life.

Why Things Happen As They Do

We are beings who require meaning. We crave to understand. The question of why things happen as they do is a subliminal question that gnaws at many. The way we answer this question determines our behavior and also our response to events. It has a great deal to do with the level of anger we live with on a daily basis and with our overall peace of mind.

Many feel that if they understood why things happen as they do, they could have some control over events. They could then use their energy wisely, make proper choices, and take the right turn in the road. When we do not know what will happen, or why it is happening, it is natural to feel insecure. This insecurity prompts many individuals to develop different ways of explaining and interpreting the events that take place in their lives.

If we believe that all is divinely ordained and takes place as it is meant to, then we do not have such a personal sense of failure when things do not go our way. If we believe that forces of karma are working, then when something difficult happens we understand it to be the effect of our own actions, thoughts, or deeds. This provides a larger context to place the events in. When something negative happens to us, we can see it as balancing out bad karma of the past, balancing the scales. In this manner, that which is negative is transformed into the positive. If we believe that we are here to learn lessons, then no matter what happens to us, it is positive because it has happened in order to teach us something and thus to strengthen us.

Active and Passive Responses

Certain points of view will lead to a positive, proactive lifestyle. Others can lead to depression, chaos, and nihilism. If we believe that life is divinely ordained or directed by karma, rather than feeling like leaves in the wind or like the victim of dark forces, we will feel empowered to respond to hardship constructively. Not only will we respond constructively, but the actions we take in our lives will be part of creating new karma for us and producing new, positive consequences. We will be mindful of what we do, knowing that negative actions will sooner or later reverberate upon ourselves. However, if we believe events are random or the outcome of sheer bad luck, we can respond with great pain and anguish, behaving in a random, angry, chaotic way—lashing out.

Today's Diet
MAKE FRIENDS WITH YOUR DESTINY

Many of us have not taken time to really think about our destiny, to see how we basically feel about it, or what are the causes of the events that go on in our lives. It can be enormously enlightening and instructive to see how we perceive this. A great deal of hidden resentment and anger toward the blows of fate can be released when we think of destiny differently. We can also become truly empowered in the way we receive the events that have taken place.

STEP 1: *Why Things Happen As They Do.*

Sit down and take some time to write a few pages about why you think events have unfolded in your life the way they have. Many of us have been taught different belief systems that deal with this question. In this exercise, you are taking a moment to see how *you* truly feel about this question—not what you have been taught to think. Often we accept certain teachings consciously, but deep down have a very different point of view. It is helpful to be true to yourself now and see what you truly believe.

STEP 2: *Whom Do You Answer To?*

To whom do you feel you are accountable in life? Do you feel your actions have consequences? Is someone judging your behavior? Take some time to look at this. When we feel we are accountable and yet cannot be thought well of, much anger and futility reside within.

STEP 3: *Forgiveness.*

Are you willing to accept forgiveness for your wrongs? Is there something you need to do to balance the scales, so you can accept forgiveness? Will you do it?

Are you willing to forgive yourself and others?

Forgiveness is the basis of all goodwill, healing, and creativity. When we can find a way to accept our hurts, disappointments, and betrayals, to offer forgiveness and understand them in a new light, our life takes on a new force. There is no better medicine than forgiveness. There is no worse poison than retaining hurts and anger within.

When You Are the Recipient of Anger

He who has control over his tongue
is greater than a hero in battle.

— Shivananda

Many live their lives fearing criticism, rejection, ostracism, humiliation, deceit, or other forms of attack by others. They actually fashion their lives around ways to defend themselves against it. Oddly enough, the more we defend ourselves against something, the more we have it in our lives. When we are constantly thinking about something (even though we are thinking of ways to avoid it), we are holding it in our minds. When something is on our minds frequently, whether in a positive or negative regard, we draw it to ourselves.

The Fear of Being Harmed

The fear of being harmed or fooled by others constricts our lives enormously. It causes us to close our hearts and become distrustful, suspicious, possessive, and on the alert for schemes. This is living a life in a prison without bars.

Mary had been made to feel like a fool by her mother over and over again. Her mother publicly shamed her and laughed at all her mishaps. No matter what Mary did, her mother made fair game of it. As Mary grew up she became determined never to have this happen again. The anger she felt with her mother became converted into many walls that Mary lived her life behind.

She was not forthcoming with anyone about her personal feelings or life. Mary was present in body only, playing a role of being pert, cute, and cheerful. Deep within, she had no idea at all of what it meant to be a friend. She could not trust herself or others with anything that was meaningful to her.

When it became time for Mary to have romantic relationships, they only lasted a short while. She could not and would not express any real feelings or allow anyone to get close to her. This fear of being hurt and rejected had gripped Mary deeply and brought her that which she most dreaded. Her boyfriends withdrew and rejected her. The same thing happened with others, due to what seemed like her coldness and lack of caring.

The Best Defense Against Being Hurt

Except in the case of being physically harmed, it is important to realize that no one can hurt us unless we agree to it.

The words, deeds, and actions of others in and of themselves do not hurt. It is what they mean to us, the way we receive them and interpret them that causes the pain and sorrow.

The best defense against being hurt is to feel good about ourselves, to be centered in the truth of our lives, who we are, what we give, and our true value. We must realize that the way a person responds to us says much more about them than it does about us. Just because a specific person rejects us does not mean that we are not lovable and worthy of being cared for. The person rejects us for reasons of their own. They may be afraid of intimacy. They may have had other experiences that are getting in their way now. We suffer not because of their actions, but because of what we make it mean in our lives. We go into agreement with the negativity they are expressing and feel we deserve it, that they are right. We validate their point of view, rather than look within and adopt our own vision of who we are and validate that.

Causes of Being Hurt by Others

When someone in whom I have placed much love,
time and value rejects and betrays me,
may I regard him as a great, sacred friend.

— SHANTIDEVA

Once again we come across this unique saying. It is well worth pondering. Why would we regard someone who has deeply disappointed us as a great, sacred friend? What is being pointed to here is the suggestion to look more deeply into the very nature of relationships. Perhaps the hurt we receive in relationships comes from a failure to understand the essential nature of our lives and the purpose of our relationships.

This quotation helps us understand that we are not hurt by others, but by our attachment to them, and to the way in which we demand that the relationship develop. We all have many expectations about how others should behave, who they must be, and the ways in which they must requite our kindness to them. These expectations are what hurt us, these personal demands. Rather than allowing each person to be who they are, and to honor the time we have together, we build an entire edifice describing what others must be for us. This is not truly being with another, but using them as an object to fulfill our own needs. This attitude, sooner or later, always leads to disappointment and pain.

When we learn to give and receive and to love unconditionally, just valuing and appreciating each person as they come and go, the pain we have will dissolve. The best defense is always love.

Impermanence

The Buddha has said that all composite things must dissolve. All those who meet will have to part. All those who love will have to say good-bye. This is the nature of human life itself. When we understand the fundamental rhythm of life and do not try to hold on to that which is here only temporarily, when we honor each person's right to be exactly who they are and not live their life to please us, the pain, hurt, and anger we feel will be greatly diminished. As we do this we will also get in touch with the greater law of oneness, and personally realize that the love we share never disappears, but goes on forever in different ways.

Today's Diet
LOOK THROUGH THE EYES OF LOVE

A clenched fist cannot hit a smiling face.

When we fear harm, when we see negativity in others, we draw it forth. When we look for the best in others, focus upon what we have in common, how we can help, what we can give, we bring forth a positive response. Take charge of the way you see others. Learn to respond, not to react.

STEP 1: *Stop Reacting Blindly.*

Automatic, instinctive reactions to attack never work in the long run. Take a moment and see where and when you are most vulnerable to reacting blindly. These are your danger spots. Learn to pause at these moments. Breathe deeply. Look away from the person. Say to yourself, "Just like me, this person wants to be happy. Just like me, this person fears suffering."

Give yourself much-needed time. This is a pause that alters the very nature of your life.

STEP 2: *Respond Differently.*

Responsibility means having the ability to respond. This is what it means to be human and to live a life from the highest and best part of ourselves. When we respond we are choosing the way we want to view this particular person and situation. We are living from our own values and standards, not those of someone else.

Decide how you want to respond. Decide who you want to be. Decide what is meaningful to you and live on the basis of that.

STEP 3: *Look Through the Eyes of Love.*

When we love and care for someone, no matter what they say or do, we see it differently than if we viewed them as the enemy. We all have the innate ability to choose to see the best about the person, to stop and truly listen to what they have to say. We have the ability to give them the benefit of the doubt, and to communicate our own feelings and thoughts carefully and without blame or attack. Because someone is negative toward us does not mean we have to respond in kind. We have the choice of whether or not we wish to bathe ourselves in anger or in love.

Take a moment and close your eyes. Look at yourself through the eyes of someone who loves you. Then, look at yourself through your own eyes. What's the difference? How did it feel to be looked at through the eyes of love?

Do this exercise every day with someone. Take a moment to realize that the way you look at that person affects them. Carefully and consciously, look at them through the eyes of love.

Review and Repair

Today's Diet
REVIEW OF THE PAST FOUR DAYS

STEP 1: *The Most Meaningful Ideas*

Write down the most meaningful ideas of the past four days to you. What about them touched you?

STEP 2: *The Most Meaningful Exercises*

Which exercises were most meaningful to you? Why? Would you like to make some adjustments to them? It's fine. Do it. It's wonderful to take what suits you and fine-tune it. We are all different. A little adjustment here or there makes it your own.

STEP 3: *The Most Difficult Exercises*

Which exercises were most difficult? Were there some you could not or would not do? That's fine as well. It's to be expected. It's also extremely valuable to notice which ones they were. Take a little while to reflect upon this. What was it about these exercises that was so difficult or unpleasant to you? Can you see how doing them might make a difference in your life? Would you be willing to try even one of them? Would you be willing to do one today?

STEP 4: *The Most Meaningful Interaction*

As we undertake these exercises, new and meaningful interactions take place. It is inevitable. Write down what happened to you. Describe your meaningful interactions. What else happened between you and others? It's good to keep a record. As we go through this program it will become fascinating to look back and follow the trail we have gone along.

STEP 5: *Changes That Are Needed*

Write what changes you notice are needed in your life as you have gone through these past few days. Don't be afraid to write down anything that you think of. You will not have to do them all at once. Just make a note of them. Simply realizing that changes are needed is a huge step. Most of us don't take time to pay attention to this. Acknowledge yourself for being willing to be aware of changes that may need to take place.

STEP 6: *Actions That Are Needed*

As we do these exercises we can become aware of people we haven't called or contacted, gifts we haven't given, projects we've left unfinished, dreams we've left unfulfilled. It's helpful to write these down. Just make a list. Don't become overwhelmed by it. Just write it down.

STEP 7: *Changes That Have Taken Place*

As we go through these days we will also become aware of natural, spontaneous changes that have taken place in the way we see things and relate to others. Write these down. They're fascinating. Many happen all by themselves.

STEP 8: *Actions That Have Taken Place*

Just as changes have naturally taken place, we most likely have taken many new actions. Keep a record of these. It is very easy for things we do to slip away. If we do not take time to notice and record our actions, they escape our view. The more we notice and become aware of what is going on, the more power it has in our lives and the lives of others. We also receive encouragement and inspiration by taking time to realize and absorb what is happening.

STEP 9: *New Possibilities*

Here is our chance to write down any new steps we may wish to take. Anything can be included, in any area of our lives. As we go through this program, new desires, goals, hopes, and possibilities will be arising. Don't let them slip away. What are the new possibilities that are appearing on your horizon? Write them down. Give them life.

STEP 10: *New Promises*

Do you want to make a promise to yourself today? This is a strong resolution that is important to you. Promises have power. Keeping a promise is even more empowering than making one. Start off by making a promise you can keep. See how it feels to keep it.

STEP 11: *Wins*

Here is the place where you list your gains in well-being. The mind naturally wants to negate change, progress, and new steps. By taking time to review and repair what is going on we turn that process around. We acknowledge what we are doing and what its consequences are in our lives. As you do this, you will be amazed at how many ways you win. What you focus upon increases, and the more you focus upon your wins, not your losses, the more they will appear in your life.

Happy sailing.

Maintenance

To care for things makes the whole world come to life.

— ZEN SAYING

MOST OF US would never go out in the morning without taking a shower, brushing our teeth, combing our hair, and preparing to meet the world. However, we usually pay little attention to purifying and preparing our hearts and minds. We go forth feeling any old way, and allow our passing moods and impulses to rule the day.

These exercises are cumulative. When we do them regularly, they become part of our flesh and bones. Before long our experience changes as does our feelings about ourselves. However, it is absolutely crucial to keep it going and do some exercises every day. If we do not take charge of how we think, feel, and act, others will be only too happy to do so.

It is important to allot a certain amount of time each day to reviewing the exercises and choosing which ones to practice that day. It is good to do this at the same time each day so that it becomes a habit. Just as we wouldn't go out without our morning coffee, eventually we won't want to go out without our inner exercises. (This can be done in the evening as well, of course).

All through our days and lives, we are barraged by endless challenges and negativity. We need to build inner muscles to be able to maintain the state of mind where we do not respond blindly or allow negativity to take hold. In order to build these muscles and maintain them, mindful attention to the exercises is a must. Before long, you'll feel so good doing them that you won't be able to imagine living the old way again.

I am going to suggest a maintenance program. You are free to make your own. Experiment and see how it works for you. It is also wonderful to do this program with a friend or a group of friends. There is nothing like the support of others to keep one's inspiration alive. You can choose to meet weekly to review the text and exercises and discuss what's happening in your life. Or you can have an Anger Diet buddy, someone you check in with regularly, either in person or over the phone. However you wish to arrange it, remember, the power of like minds focused on a common goal is hard to beat.

MAINTENANCE PROGRAM

STEP 1: *Take a Break.*

After you have gone through the 30 days of the Anger Diet, take 2 or 3 days off. Keep a journal during those days, noting what's going on in your life and how you feel about it.

STEP 2: *Revisit the Early Stages of the Anger Diet.*

Now, go back to day 1. Choose one or two of the exercises and start all over again. This time it will be quite different. You will have changed and so will your experience. Different exercises may be more meaningful to you now. You will be amazed at many new discoveries.

STEP 3: *Proceed Day by Day.*

Choose exercises that feel right now.

STEP 4: *Get an Anger Diet Buddy.*

Find someone (or a group) who would like to share this journey with you. Not only will your relationship with that person be very joyful, but both of you will grow in strength.

STEP 5: *Keep This Process Going.*

Keep a record of the exercises that are most relevant for you, and the ones that are most difficult as well. Go back to those for a week or two. Then begin all over again.

Once you have repeated the 30-day program two or three times, you will not be the same person. Write to me and let me know the ways you have changed. Consider coming to an Anger Diet Workshop, where a larger group works on these exercises together. Share the work with a friend. Give yourself a wonderful gift. You deserve it. You've come a long way.

Knowing others is wisdom.
Knowing the self is enlightenment.
Mastering others requires force.
Mastering the self needs strength.

— LAO-TZU

About the Author

Dr. Brenda Shoshanna, long-term psychologist, therapist, relationship expert, speaker, and workshop leader, is the author of many books, including *Zen and the Art of Falling in Love*, *Zen Miracles*, *Why Men Leave*, and *What He Can't Tell You and Needs to Say*. A frequent media guest on national television, she is the relationship expert on iVillage.com and an instructor on BarnesandNobleUniversity.com. She lives in Manhattan and is available for counseling, speaking, and workshops. You may contact her at topspeaker@yahoo.com or her personal Web site, www.brendashoshanna.com. You may learn more about *The Anger Diet* and find additional resources at her Web site www.theangerdiet.com.